Reiki and Christ-Based Healing

Differences and Dangers

Reiki and Christ-Based Healing

Differences and Dangers

Rhonda J. McClenton

Ichthus Press, LLC
Bala Cynwyd, Pennsylvania

Ichthus Press LLC
PO Box 35
Bala Cynwyd, PA 19004-0035

© 2011 by Rhonda J. McClenton
All Rights Reserved. Published 2011

ISBN 978-0-9833068-0-1

Library of Congress Control Number: 2011901922

Designed by Kitty Werner, RSBPress, LLC, Waitsfield, Vermont
Cover photo © bastan - Fotolia.com

Disclaimer: The information and reference materials contained here are intended solely for the general information of the reader. It is not intended to diagnose health problems or to take the place of professional medical care. Neither the publisher nor the individual author shall be liable for any physical, psychological, emotional, financial, or commercial damages, including, but not limited to, special, incidental, consequential or other damages. Our views and rights are the same: You are responsible for your own choices, actions, and results.

Use of Fictitious Names: This book is based on actual facts. Names given are pseudonyms to protect privacy of those interviewed.

Permissions: Scripture quotations marked (NIV) are taken from the Holy Bible, New International Version®, NIV®. Copyright © 1973, 1978, 1984 by Biblica, Inc.™ Used by permission of Zondervan. All rights reserved worldwide. www.zondervan.com

"Scripture taken from THE MESSAGE ©1993, 1994, 1995, 1996, 2000, 2001, 2002. Used by permission of NavPress Publishing Group"

Contents

Preface	7
Part One — Introduction to Reiki Research	**9**
Introduction to Reiki Research	11
The Reiki Experience	31
Reiki Roots	37
Tracing Reiki Energy Origins	49
A Beginning of All Things?	59
A Pantheistic Worldview	71
Therapeutic Touch: If it Quacks like a Duck…	75
Psychic Soil: Therapeutic Touch Roots	80
Reiki Claims Based on Research: Shield or Achilles' Tendon?	87
Part Two — You Shall Know The Truth…	**99**
Introduction to Biblical Healing	101
The Christ-based Healing Experience	111
Biblical Healing Roots: Observing the Source and Why Jesus Healed	115
The Miracles of Jesus in Relationship to the Laying-On of Hands	129
A Biblical Worldview	146
Part Three — You Shall Know Them by their Fruit	**151**
The Myth of Reiki Safety	153
The Reality of Biblical Healing	184
Setting Captives Free	192
My Journey: In and Out of Reiki: A New Beginning	198
Resources Cited	205
Index	213
About the Author	219

Preface

Several decades ago, I recall going on a white water rafting trip with some college friends. I had never rafted but reasoned the experience would be fun. I remember my mother being very concerned and asking, "Can you swim?" My response was that in the rapids, being able to float was far more important than being able to swim. Off I raced to my adventure assuring my mother that I would be fine. As we all donned wet suits and flotation devices, the guide alluded to potential risks and rules for safety. On the inside, I could feel butterflies preparing to dance as my raft mates talked about the thrill of steering into rocks and capsizing the raft. Too late to get out, I breathed a silent pray. For now, I would just "Go with the flow." God heard my mother's and my prayer. Out of nowhere it seemed, the guide to lead the trip jumped on my raft. While on the inside, I was breathing a sigh of relief, my weekend warrior raft mates were disgruntled. The guide was going to "spoil all the fun." Needless to say, I did not care. What mattered most is that I would arrive at my destination safe because of the guide's presence. He knew the river.

I have penned this narrative out of concern for those involved with a type of energy healing called Reiki. In most of the literature and anecdotal stories, it is being lauded as a safe and harmless intervention. It has even been presented as similar to the laying-on of hands used by biblical Jesus. However, if Reiki is being compared to healing that biblical Jesus used, then Reiki must be looked at through the lens of the Bible. For some, that may seem narrow and restrictive. However, if pointing to Scripture can be used as a reason for practicing Reiki, it can certainly be examined to discern if what is being practiced represents the truth of Christ-based healing. I recognize that in a post-modern world, "truth" has become very subjective. Individuals are quick to point out, "Your truth is not necessarily my truth." I must confess early on, I don't purport to espouse my own personal brand of truth. Yet, as both a

Christian and a minister, I do seek to point out the objective truth of God's Word.

To that end, I went on a healing journey. In seeking to better understand Reiki and Christ-based healing, I participated in a doctoral program in which three years were spent in the field connecting with practitioners of Reiki and other healing modalities. We talked; we argued; we broke bread. Before any of that happened, however, I had to listen…to their stories…to their concerns…to their questions. At the same time, I had to dig deeper into my own faith. Where were the people who experienced Christ-based healing? What did that look like? How did it feel? Were they having experiences that were different than what the practitioners had told me? I wanted to know…I needed to know.

Beyond those stories, there was the literature on Reiki and Christ-based hands-on healing. I digested every relevant journal to make sense of all the claims. This book represents the shortened and hopefully accessible version of the original research, Spirits of the Lesser Gods. It combines a personal story with the voices of "healers," recipients, and the literature examined through the grid of Scripture.

In writing this book, what are my hopes? My hope is that it will give every reader the tools to make informed decisions. My hope is that individuals will not be dismissive about warnings concerning Reiki because they have not had a particular experience. My hope is that readers will understand that in healing, there is a real distinction between being assisted by various psychic phenomena and being assisted by the Holy Spirit. Finally my hope for Reiki practitioners and recipients is that on your healing journey, the Source of true healing, who knows life's rivers will guide you to safety.

In closing, I acknowledge and thank all the "midwives" who encouraged me to find my voice and tell the story again. You know who you are.

Rhonda J. McClenton, Ph.D.
2011

Part One

Introduction to Reiki Research

Introduction to Reiki Research   1

I

My Initiation

I encountered Reiki by accident, literally. I had no idea that a freak accident would so alter my destiny, but it did. On the surface, the accident seemed to be a case of classic whiplash precipitated by being hit from behind. One day later, I found myself in the office of Dr. Virgil Hartman (all names used are pseudonyms). I knew him for about a decade but only at a distance. My visits to him were infrequent, usually two to three times a year for routine checkups and annual bouts with upper respiratory infections. There was always pleasant conversation followed by a "keep up the good work, dear." I liked him. Dr. Hartman was a bright and capable physician who normally had the ability to put me at ease. His gentleness reminded me of the bedside manner of the television physician from the seventies, Marcus Welby, M.D.

During this particular visit, his normally bright green eyes were pensive and concerned. As he examined me, he expressed concern about an area in my neck and shoulders that seemed to indicate a level of damage and extreme tension. He suggested that I take a week off just to rest. He knew that I had a very demanding job, and he was aware of the fact that I was a workaholic and would normally return to work even if I was in pain. This time I heeded his advice; I intended to rest. However, my rest was short-lived. By the middle of that week off, I found myself in a lot of pain. It was strange because the pain was both physical and emotional. While my head throbbed with nauseating headaches, I found myself crying profusely. This was unusual for me. I was so alarmed that I called Dr. Hartman. He told me to come in immediately.

"How are you feeling?"

"I'm not feeling quite myself."

"Tell me, what's been going on with you?"

"I've been feeling weepy and emotional; the thought of going back to work terrifies me." I had been under a tremendous amount of stress at work for about a year, but I internalized my stress and simply continued to work. However, the accident forced me to acknowledge how deeply affected I had become by it. His next comment floored me. It was a discussion I had with myself, but I never had talked to Dr. Hartman about it.

"You need to go. Don't you get it? This accident is divine. You've got to get your joy back. You've been robbed of your joy. You've lost your mission, and you need to take time to rediscover your mission and heal. I will help you."

Yes, the accident was a divine appointment. I had been in a stressful situation for such a long time that my system was reacting both physically and emotionally. Dr. Hartman had observed me over time, and he was familiar with the organization and the work I had done there. He discerned what I had not been able to discern initially. My mission at this particular job was over. I knew that internally, but letting go seemed like I was abandoning my post.

However, I grew to realize that after a ten-year journey at one place, I was now in need of healing, both physical and emotional. If I did not get the necessary rest, the tension that had somehow become lodged in my neck and shoulders and caused mild concussive symptoms would continue. I reasoned that I could take medication for the headaches, but there was no pill to extinguish the emotional overload. I took a three-month medical leave and resigned. The generous severance package given by my company allowed me to rest for about a year.

For weeks, Dr. Hartman asked me the same questions, "How is your spirit? How's your soul?" He seemed deeply interested in my healing. He talked a lot about treating the whole person and not just symptoms or maladies. While initially I felt that he was simply extending a professional courtesy, in time I grew to recognize that his interactions with me were much more than professional niceties.

In about six months, I had fully recuperated. God had used Dr. Hartman to facilitate healing in my own life. The healing that came about was both physical and emotional. When I was no longer under Dr. Hartman's care, we became friends. I later found out that he had observed and admired my professional commitment to helping others and my relationship with God. While I could not recall any in-depth conversations about God, he saw God reflected in my lifestyle. That relationship drew him towards me. As I became better acquainted with him, I recognized that he too was in need of healing—emotional, physical, and spiritual.

II

We made plans to meet at a Borders Book Store on Resurrection Sunday after we both had attended our respective churches. His eyes glistened as he shared with me his premise about sickness and disease. "Although I am a doctor and I treat a lot of ailments, I believe that many of man's problems are spiritual." He concluded that when a person's life was out of balance, sickness and disease resulted. I was surprised at his insight. He was a physician; I initially expected him to be more Cartesian than spiritual. He was an interesting blend of both. As we talked, he shared openly about his life, his failures, and his aspirations. He talked so much about healing and spirituality that I wondered where he actually stood in his relationship with God.

"Virgil, what faith are you?" A wry smile crossed his face. It was an innocent question.

"I guess you might say that I'm Christian. I'm also a Methodist; however, I am starting to believe that reincarnation might be true." I remembered thinking how odd it was that he could believe in reincarnation since he talked about being a Christian. I pressed him.

"So, Virgil, where *are* you spiritually?" He paused for a moment.

"I guess I'm on my path. You know that there are many paths, but they all lead to God."

I shook my head. "Yes, there are many paths, but I don't think that they all lead to God."

His smile told me that this conversation was a familiar one for him. The pregnant silence indicated that for now, we both wisely decided to agree to disagree. Through sips of coffee and cappuccino, we talked about what our passions were. I shared with him that my deep passion was getting people connected to God. I smiled when he articulated that he shared a similar desire. He felt quite strongly that his life assignment was to get people connected spiritually.

To that end, he invited me to an event that he was hosting at his home. It was an open house featuring the "healing work of eighteen practitioners." The practitioners included body workers who specialized in Massage and Polarity Therapy, Shiatsu, Alexander Technique, Acupressure, Acupuncture, Chiropractic, and Therapeutic Touch. It was in this context that I first heard about Reiki. Many of the practitioners talked about "balancing energy" and doing "energy work." Some touted the benefits of Chinese herbs and homeopathy. The gathering was attended by hundreds of individuals interested in healing. For all intents and purposes, it was a success.

However, I was very perplexed. I kept hearing about healing, but I never heard anything about God or Jesus. I left this setting curious, but I was also now concerned for Virgil. He was genuinely interested in the healing of others; I had seen that demonstrated in my own life. However, the healing modalities that I observed seemed incongruent with what I knew about Christian healing. An opportunity would soon present itself for me to find out more.

III

At Virgil's insistence, I traveled to Israel. He thought that the trip would help me further recuperate and hear clearly from God about my next assignment. Frequently in our previous conversations, he queried me about my next step. I told him that I honestly did not know. He assured me that God would speak to me in Israel. What amazed me was that although his spiritual path seemed riddled with ambiguity and contradictions, he still possessed some spiritual insight as it related to the lives of others.

I recalled walking along a dusty road on the outskirts of Jerusalem. The area looked like a desert place. I remembered my pastor referencing I Kings (17:3) and alluding to the fact that this location was where the prophet Elijah was sent and fed by a raven. What was so strange was that, as my pastor shared this insight, a raven actually appeared in the sky. It was a powerful metaphor highlighting God's provision in the wilderness. Stranger still was that, although the area appeared barren, we suddenly came across a small patch of bright reddish orange flowers. From a distance, they actually appeared to be on fire, almost like a burning bush. I was so deeply moved by the incident that I took a picture.

IV

As I stood at the Wailing Wall among thousands of pilgrims, many rocking back and forth wailing and many bowing prostrate in silent prayer, I stuck a piece of paper in the crevice of the massive brick wall. It was a note to God asking not only for my own clarity and direction but also for clarity about what role I was to play in Virgil's life. I was exposed to the open house for a reason. I was privy to seeing the demonstration of various healing arts, but I was unclear about what I was to do with the information. I clearly felt that Virgil was a deeply spiritual man, but I also felt that something was amiss in the healing modalities I had witnessed. By the end of my stay in Israel, God gave me the clarity and direction I sought.

V

"So, did God speak to you in Israel?" Virgil inquired. His green eyes twinkled, and his arms were folded across his chest. A knowing smile surfaced on his face. Although we sat in a crowded sun-lit café, the din of the room seemed far away and the space felt very private, almost sacred. In response, I nodded. The question seemed rhetorical, as he did not wait for additional information. "You know, you were in the land of antiquity. I hope that you learned something about patience. Some things take time to develop."

"Am I impatient?"

He laughed at my question. "Is a school bus yellow?"

Actually, I was. Even as I sought God for direction, I wanted Him to give me a complete road map. I had not shared that with Virgil, but somehow he knew. At that point, however, I did not tell him what I thought God said concerning my direction. However, I gave him the picture I took in the desert. The color momentarily emptied from his face.

"Where did you get this from?" I explained that it was from Israel. "What day and time was this taken?" I mentally searched for the exact date and time and finally turned the picture over which highlighted the date. He shook his head and whispered, "It's the burning bush." I sat in my seat, stirred and awe-struck at the same time; I reflected on God's call to Moses. If there were more words spoken, I could not recall them.

VI

He was between patients but wanted to grab a quick bite. He apologized for the setting but promised that the food was good. It was in a tavern that was situated in an upscale area; nevertheless, it was still a tavern. He slowly sipped his beer. "So, what did God say to you in Israel?" He picked up where our last conversation had ended. He seemed anxious; I was nervous. I did not know that today was the day to reveal to him what I had heard in Israel.

"Actually, I heard two things. The first was that I was to pray for you, I mean intense prayer; it's called intercessory prayer." He smiled.

"I could certainly use lots of prayer.

"The second was that I was to volunteer some time to assist you." He nodded in agreement as if he had already read the script. He cleared his throat and gazed directly at me.

"My sense is that I am to serve as a catalyst in your life. You've got some good skills in the area of administration, and you are spiritual. I could use your help as a volunteer administrator as I seek to pull this group of healers together. I need to be able to let them know that healing is done by the Spirit. That's what I've been called to do." Thus began my assignment with Dr. Virgil Hartman. He was a man of many paradoxes. Spiritually, he appeared to be on a wilderness journey in terms of his relationship with a personal God; yet in that desert, there were signs of spiritual vitality and hunger. Yes, I would have to trust God on this new journey, for I could not trace him.

VII

Virgil introduced me to the group as a volunteer administrator and his spiritual advisor. While some members of this Healing Circle were warm and accepting, one member eyed me suspiciously. Her name was Shalimar. I overheard her as she pulled Virgil aside, "Why is she here?" Once again, he repeated what he had publicly stated. The disgruntled look on her face indicated that she perceived me as a threat. Instinctively, I felt uncomfortable around her. In time, I recognized that while Virgil was the formal head of the group, she actually was the informal leader. She was usually flanked by one or two women who were Reiki-masters. At that point, I still did not know what a Reiki-master was. What I did know is that she ran workshops where Reiki was performed. Aside from occasional greetings, she kept her distance with me.

For months, I attended several meetings and gave Virgil feedback after the meetings. I rarely said anything during the meetings; I just observed. The purpose of the meetings seemed to be to familiarize each member of the group with what the others did. Afterward, a demonstration followed with someone volunteering from the group. The goal of the group was also to network, which would allow members to receive new referrals. The meetings always ended with a meal. Initially, I attempted to be open-minded. I knew that I needed to learn about what these healers were doing. However, over time, I grew increasingly uncomfortable as I heard more about mystical energies, balancing the chakras, and the interconnectedness of all things. I remember feeling sick one day as one of the group members excitedly talked about building a sweat lodge on her property. What disturbed me was her claim that the information was channeled to her from an Egyptian king who had been dead for several millennia. I literally felt my skin crawl. I confronted Virgil after the meal.

"Virgil, Laura said that she got plans for a sweat lodge from channeling." A winsome smile crossed his face.

"I guess God works in mysterious ways," he retorted. I was not amused.

"That's not how God works," I chided. Still, he dismissed the whole incident. I knew that channeling was forbidden by God as an occult practice. I began to sense that my time of observation was ending. After this incident, Virgil called me in anticipation of the next meeting. I knew I needed to let him know how uncomfortable I felt.

"Virgil, I've got some real concerns about the direction of the group. Where is it going?" He thought about it for a moment.

"Actually, I'm not really sure. You know the group is still forming."

"Yes, but the purpose of the group is very ambiguous."

"Well, the role of the group is to build a network of healers that support one another and provide healing." I knew I now needed to be direct.

"Virgil, we both have talked about sharing a Christian faith. How is it that in all of these meetings we have never mentioned God or Jesus? I mean, how can we talk about healing without talking about Jesus? I keep hearing people talk about being spiritual, but God is not a part of those meetings." Virgil grew very quiet and reflective. He agreed that the focus would have to become more spiritual, but he did not tell me how that would take place. I was soon to discover that "spiritual" did not necessarily mean "Christian." A few days before the meeting, Virgil and I were to set a meeting agenda. However, after expressing his frustration about the lack of spiritual focus in the meeting to Shalimar, she suddenly came up with an agenda for the next meeting. She sent the meeting agenda to select members of the group that she could influence. Some of the more vocal group members were not informed that there would be a meeting. I received an agenda, and the focus of the meeting was now very spiritual.

The agenda of the meeting set a time for the healers to talk about the spiritual aspects of healing in their own practices. Afterwards, there was to be a series of attunements. These attunements would be followed by silence to await the arrival of "spirit." When I read the agenda in its entirety, I again had a nauseous feeling in my stomach. My skin started to crawl as it had when one of the healers talked about channeling. For whatever reason, I felt a sense of great danger. I shared my concerns with a minister friend. She immediately became alarmed and warned me about leaving the group immediately.

Initially, I was unsure what I should do. I sensed danger, but I did not know what to say to Virgil. I prayed for guidance. That evening, I visited the same Borders where Virgil and I had first talked. Instinctively, I went over to a section on Alternative Medicine. I had already begun to read a lot of the literature because my interest had been piqued from meeting with the practitioners in the Healing Circle. I now knew that much of what was practiced had ties to Eastern Mysticism and the occult. However, I wanted to suspend judgment until I had gathered enough information. That evening, I happened upon an entire collection of books on Reiki. I had never read anything on Reiki. As I perused an introductory book, I was horrified as the book talked about an initiation ceremony that was comprised of a series of attunements. The goal of the attunements was to open the individual to divine healing energy. Once initiated, the individual would become a Reiki channel. Concerning this energy, one of the books stated that an attunement opens the student's crown to receive the healing energy of Source. Once the crown was opened, the practitioner would serve as a channel, and the Source energy would flow to wherever it was needed. Other books highlighted the initiation ceremony and talked about side effects from attunement.

I wanted to run as far as I could from this Healing Circle. I did not know a lot about Reiki, but it was the antithesis of any healing I had ever heard or read about in Christian circles. Although my flight instinct was strong, I was also concerned about Virgil. How could I warn him and have him really listen? I now recognized that Virgil was a risk-taker. He did not avoid things because of biblical prohibitions; he felt that an experience would always win over an argument. In addition, it seemed that if something were spiritual and related to healing, he felt that it had to be of God. I disagreed. I prayed that God would give me wisdom in talking to Virgil.

On the day of the meeting, I decided that I would simply go to his home early and explain to him why I could not come. Because he had relationships with these healers, I tried to express myself in a way that would not offend or demonize those involved. He led me to the kitchen table and had me sit down. He could read the concern in my eyes.

"Virgil, I don't know what it is, but there is something not right about these attunements. This is not how God heals. Furthermore, the agenda talked about waiting in silence for a spirit to come. What spirit is that?" He shook his head indicating that he did not know. "Well, Virgil, whatever it is, I think it's evil." He grabbed my hands.

"I'm not involved with any evil spirits." His eyes were plaintive.

"I did not say you were, but there is something that just doesn't feel right about any of this."

"Fine, Shalimar's agenda will not be used. I will make a new one, and we will meet down here instead of the office she uses." I nodded with approval. "What people need to know is that healing is by God's Spirit. Right now, some of them are not comfortable with the concept of God. They've got the right idea but the wrong spirit. That will take time to change." I knew that the meeting would move in a different direction; God had heard my prayer.

VIII

Shalimar was one of the first to arrive. A Reiki-master was with her. Virgil explained how the agenda and the location of the meeting had been changed. Shalimar stared like a sullen child and insisted that the meeting still be held upstairs in her office. He conceded. As group members came, Shalimar directed them to her office. I could feel tension mounting, but I prayed silently under my breath.

Virgil and I were the last ones to arrive at the meeting. When we arrived, more than half of the group of ten members was sitting on overstuffed pillows on the floor. Although it was daylight, a candle and incense were burning. Many of the members sat quietly and stared at the flame in a trance-like fashion. Initially, it seemed that they had not even recognized that anyone had entered the room. Virgil opened the meeting with a brief prayer and began to share his concerns about the focus of the group. One by one, he had each member talk about the role they felt that the Spirit played in their healing work. He never said Holy Spirit, and some of the responses were ambiguous and mystical. Once everyone had shared, Virgil spoke with conviction and clarity.

"I apologize for the lack of clarity and direction that has been in the group. Things have not been clear because the vision is still evolving for me. However, the revelation that I have received is that true healing is from God and is done by his Spirit. Healing does not come from us; it comes through us. We are just vessels." It was obvious that some in the group were uncomfortable with the direction the meeting was taking. He was very aware of this. "I am not at all sure where this journey will lead me. Perhaps, I may be marching to the beat of a different drummer. If you are at a different place, that is okay." Having said that, several members of the group told Virgil that they had different needs in their healing work. They voluntarily chose to leave the group. A handful of members remained. In the months that followed, the group lost momentum.

By this time, I had done a great deal of research. I was convinced that many of the practices, especially Reiki, were spiritually dangerous. I knew that Virgil was not totally convinced. With much of the group cohesion gone, he initially sought to reinvigorate the group by having another open house. I was against this and challenged him to allow me to do a force field analysis (this tool does not measure any type of spiritual force or energy field) where I would analyze the strengths, weaknesses, opportunities, and threats of revitalizing the group. After completing the analysis, we had a lengthy discussion. I tried to highlight the healing modalities that were either safe or at least spiritually neutral. However, I warned that practices that involved channeling energy were dangerous because they involved connecting with a spiritual realm that God forbade. His question to me spoke volumes, "Can't we integrate?" I shook my head to indicate "no." The group disbanded, but some of the healers continued to rent space to practice their healing art. Shalimar came periodically and worked with a Reiki practitioner. I constantly prayed; for a season, Reiki appeared to be a non-issue. I began to think that my assignment in the field was complete. However, in time, through another set of divinely ordered circumstances, I actually came to work for Virgil as Personnel Consultant and Office Manager. While my first assignment with Virgil as a voluntary administrator gave me a general understanding of the dangers of Reiki, my three-year journey in Virgil's office was truly informative. Watching his transformation, especially in terms of his relationship to God, helped me to understand the undisclosed side effects of following the Reiki path that manifested over time. The office became the incubator for my research on Reiki.

Reiki's Debut

Throughout antiquity, many have assumed the appellation "healer." Generally, these individuals have been deeply mystical or spiritual people who claimed power from God, nature, or some other force designated to bring about healing or a relief of symptoms to the troubled person. My task is not to cite all groups of people who now designate themselves as "healers" but to deal with one group in particular—Reiki practitioners. They speak freely and candidly about their ability to shrink tumors, send cancers into remission, eradicate addictions, and reconnect dying patients to their spiritual selves.

Additionally, they have attempted to validate these claims by purporting that the method utilized, hands on healing or laying-on of hands, was the *same* method used by Jesus. Hence, schools and individuals skilled in the healing art of Reiki have materialized to initiate the thousands who had the desire to heal themselves and others. The masses included nuns, priests, housewives, nurses, shamans, psychics, and New Age channelers.

While some had very clear ties to organized religion, others reported no religious affiliations; many boldly proclaimed allegiances to groups with strong occult and metaphysical underpinnings. I began to ponder how was it possible that a shaman (medicine man or woman) could allege to have the same power displayed by Jesus? How was it plausible that a Wiccan (witch), who deified nature, yet failed to recognize the patriarchal God of the Old Testament or the Lordship of the New Testament Christ, claim access to the *same* healing power of biblical Jesus? Finally, how could a housewife who asserted no religious affiliations but talked of being "spiritual," provide hands on healing for people and still not have a relationship with either God or Jesus?

Obviously, someone has been presenting a major falsehood or a grand delusion. However, in defiance of some very apparent contradictions, the numbers of those giving or receiving Reiki have continued to explode. Miles and True (2003) in the article, "Reiki—Review of a Biofield Therapy History, Theory, Practice, and Research" reflected:

> Although Reiki was first used in lay practice, it is increasingly used in a variety of medical settings including hospice

care settings, emergency rooms, psychiatric settings, operating rooms, nursing homes, pediatric, rehabilitation, and family practice centers, obstetrics, gynecology, and neonatal care units, HIV/AIDS, and organ transplantation care units, and for a variety of medical conditions such as cancer, pain, autism/special needs, infertility, neurodegenerative disorders, and fatigue syndromes. Reiki's popularity among lay population is evidenced by its mention in a wide variety of publications from the *New York Times,* and *Time,* to *Esquire* and *Town & Country.* (Miles and True, 65)

Despite Reiki's growing acceptance, the body of Christ for the most part has remained silent or ignorant about Reiki. The fact that many have suggested that they could heal as Jesus did should arouse the concern of the body of Christ, especially those Christians (cessationists) who maintain that faith healing is *not* for today. Ankerberg and Weldon (1991, 4) asserted, "Although awareness has grown, discernment among Christians has remained marginal in the area of healthcare practices which are at one level hostile to biblical teaching." However, for those who have traveled the Reiki Path, their spiritual experiences and entrée into Reiki have been as varied as their individual backgrounds.

Darryl

Plagued by problems in adolescence, challenges in school with peers and teachers, and views of the "church" that seemed distinct from his own, nursing student Darryl Harris (1998) admitted that he had lost his sense of self by his mid-twenties. He chronicled his journey into Reiki in an honors thesis for his nursing program. He recalled:

> *When I first inquired about Reiki, I was in a relationship that was undergoing considerable strain. I had been struggling with issues of sexuality, past abuse, and a recent traumatic work experience. From the little I had learned of Reiki, from magazines*

and pamphlets, I thought it would be a solution to the compounding stress in my life that had been manifesting as sleeplessness, headaches, muscle tension, and mood fluctuations. (6)

His search led him to a clinical nurse specialist who seemed more interested in his care than financial gain. She invited him to experience Reiki. He maintained that what followed was the "most amazing thing . . . that has ever happened in my life" (3). He described in vivid detail the sensations that took place when hands were laid on his body. When the experience was over, he recalled, "It was as if I had entered some sort of four dimensional continuum. Then I became aware of a strange, yet familiar, presence. Words cannot describe accurately what I felt then, but it was a sense of closeness to something Holy, spiritual in essence, a connection or oneness with all creation" (6). That evening, he felt relaxed and slept better than he had slept in the last ten years. Convinced of Reiki's curative power, he became initiated into first degree Reiki.

Several traumatic events took place in his life pursuant to Reiki, which left him feeling "emotionally and spiritually damaged..." (4). However, Darryl had experienced a metamorphosis. "I now had the strength and courage to face what I had previously feared.... It was as if through Reiki, I had found the way to strip way the pretenses and emerge a new person.... Through my practice and study of Reiki I have come to a point where I can continue to examine and transform my life" (6).

Jeri

In her book, *Tapestry of Healing*, Jeri Mills (2001), a physician and Reiki-Master Teacher recounted how relocating to Arizona facilitated a personal journey of discovering herself. "I looked toward the etheric and the spiritual. The mountains and the desert embraced me in their magic spell. The ancient spirits of the sahuaros [large cactus] seemed to whisper my name as they welcomed me into their land" (26). Learning meditation opened a gateway to various forms of alternative healing which included shamanic journeys in which she was able to "...retrieve lost parts of herself to become whole" (26). It also led her into Native American spirituality and an interest in channeling healing energy. Her experience of being able to channel "healing" energy to a pregnant teen in labor and bring relief initiated the process of using "energy work" on other distressed patients in labor. It also made her ripe for learning Reiki and gradually integrating the practice into other aspects of western medicine. Mills recounted how she intervened with Reiki when a man was thrown from his horse. "...His left arm was cradled in his right hand...it was obvious that he was hurting. My hands heated up and I had an overwhelming urge to offer assistance....I simply presumed he would be closed to any alternative healing methods. I suspected he might even think I was crazy if I offered to lay on hands to remove his pain" (72). However, with his consent, she administered a Reiki treatment. "...The pain in his arm was relieved while I ran energy through it but returned as soon as I removed my hands." (73). Given Mills' training as a veterinarian, she eventually used Reiki on horses and other animals. In seeking permission from horse owners, she explained, "...I could not guarantee miracle cures, but I could assure them that Reiki would cause no harm" (83).

Edward

Edward by his own admission was a marginal born-again Christian when he became involved with Reiki. However, his involvement did not result from him going to get initiated; he may not have gone that route. His came as a result of a massage.

In reflecting on his journey into Reiki, he shared about reconnecting with a woman he had been attracted to prior to his marriage. She was from Germany and visited his parents while in the states. Edward and Susie went golfing together. Because of the outing, he developed lower back pain and asked his friend to give him a massage. He recalled:

> *There was still this lust that I've carried from my youth and I [got] this chance to be alone with her and to have her*

work on my back, and that's the open door. That was the open door that when she was massaging my back, she came to that point on my back, toward my lower back, and she spread her thumbs, that spirit of Reiki filled me. And I mean filled me in such a way that I could feel it flow from where her fingers touched me all the way down to my toes, to my finger tips to the top of my head, I was filled with this <u>energy</u>, an overwhelming energy. It just blew me away. That's what set me on the point of 'I wanted more, I had to have more, I had to find out what causes this. I would have to find out where it came from. I had to have this.' And I walked around for probably a month feeling like I had all this excess energy from somewhere, and I had to find out more about it.

[I commented that it sounded like being high.]

It was very much like being—like being high, but clear-minded. It was definitely the energy of this demonic spirit. It entered me at that point...my spirit was opened up and that demon entered. My focus was really on that energy, on the source of that energy. That particular demon was the focus of my desires at that point....I begged her for where this was, what this was because after that—after that initial experience, I was able to work on my wife's back and just by running my thumbs down it, align her spine. She would hear the pop; she could feel it. Now I was practicing Reiki....[The] part that didn't make sense to most people in Reiki was [Susie] was not a Reiki Master that did it. Typically, it has to be a Reiki Master and the Reiki Master has to do it at a level one ceremony. There was no ceremony. But I was so open and she was so full of this spirit that she was able to just give it to me. My attunement came then. My changes came then. Typically, I don't know how they've told you about a Reiki one experience....But one of the first things they told us when you go to your Reiki one attunement is that you will have physical changes. Body fluids will change. Some people feel like they're sick. Their body chemistry changes after their initial receiving of this demon. That happened for me at that incident. At that massage when I received the energy of that demon, everything—everything changed. The smell of my sweat, the excrements, both kinds, uh, even sexual excrement—everything changed. I mean gelled, changed color, changed smell, everything changed in me....It changed my body chemistry so radically, as I say every excrement became foul. It was scary. But I hadn't gone to a Reiki one meeting in which they would tell you that things could change. It just changed. And it blew me away. I suddenly had the power of that demon and I went through the physical changes.... I found a Reiki Master [and two schools]....One school really treated it as a science, tried to make it into like a scientific-like practice. [It's] the same thing that happens at Transcendental Meditation; they try to take it out of the spirit realm and—make it a pseudo-science. The other [school] was the Reiki Alliance. Well, the Reiki Alliance went into the softness, the kindness, the spirit side of it, the—and I knew this is what I had. What I had wasn't a cold science. What I had had a spiritual dimension to it...." In becoming officially initiated, he remembered, *"It made no change in me whatsoever to go through the ceremony because I had already received the spirit of Reiki...[I was] able to use its powers, falling under its spell."* [I asked Edward if he still considered himself a Christian at this point.] *"I was a deceived Christian....When that lust for power came in, that had me surrendered..., [I] was ready to give up everything and anything....I think the biggest thing was that to have more of that energy, I was willing to compromise anything."* [When he asked Reiki Masters about his bodily changes, he commented,] *"The Reiki Masters explain away by the fact that, 'Oh, it's cleansing.' [But actually]...your body is adjusting to that presence."*

Reiki Defined

Having now read some brief initial experiences by Reiki practitioners, the question for many may remain, "Exactly what is Reiki?" Reiki is a Japanese word that combines two syllables: "rei" which is defined as "universal" and "ki" which means "life force." William Rand, Reiki Master and Director of the International Center for Reiki Training asserted:

> The word "rei" as it is used in Reiki is more accurately interpreted to mean supernatural knowledge or spiritual consciousness. This wisdom comes from God or the Higher Self. This is the God Consciousness that is all-knowing. It understands each person completely....
>
> Ki means the same as "Chi" in Chinese, "Prana" in Sanskrit and "Ti" in Hawaiian....Ki is used by martial artists in their physical training and mental development. It is used in meditative breathing exercises called Pranyamas and by the shamans in all cultures for divination, psychic awareness, manifestation and healing. Ki is the non-physical energy used by all healers. Ki is present all around and can be accumulated by the mind....
>
> ...It is the God-consciousness called "Rei" that guides the life force called "Ki" in the practice we call Reiki. Therefore, Reiki can be defined as spiritually guided life force energy....Reiki guides itself with its own wisdom and being unresponsive to the direction of the practitioner. (1999, n.p.)

What is so disturbing about this "healing power" is that it is the same force behind occult practices that God prohibits, and yet supporters have had no difficulty ascribing that same power to Jesus. The Bible is replete with God's prohibitions against trafficking in the spirit realm. In Deuteronomy 18:9-12, God was very clear when he warned the Israelites about occult practices. He admonished them not to be involved with divination, mediums, charmers, or wizards because they were an abomination to him. However, in the practice of Reiki that involved mediumship, the warnings of the Bible were ignored. One major reason for ignoring biblical prohibitions was that many practitioners embraced worldviews that were distinct from a biblical worldview. Moreover, a part of Reiki's acceptance was tied to the repackaging of this occult practice for western audiences. In its presentation at retreat centers, seminars, and even churches, Reiki appeared innocuous.

The Reiki Experience 2

Reiki Training

If one were to watch a movie to become more informed about the practice of Reiki, he or she would discover that there are actually two primary actors: one is the Reiki practitioner and the other is the recipient. Reiki is a healing intervention for which one must be initiated. Thus, a person who wants to practice Reiki has the option of being trained on three different levels. Generally, the Reiki aspirant will seek out a Reiki Master who has been initiated into all three levels and can now transmit Reiki energy to the student. Initiation into each level can take place over the span of a weekend in a retreat-like setting or any atmosphere that is conducive to holding what for many becomes a "sacred ceremony" replete with rituals and secrecy. At each level, it is suggested that the practitioner spend time doing "healing work" on a particular level before advancing to the next.

Level One

At level one, the main goal is to be "opened up" to channel Reiki energy. To facilitate this process, participants are told about the history and objectives of Reiki. After the background is explained, participants are given a series of four attunements. Attunement is what sets Reiki apart from other energy modalities. "Attunement into Reiki is a physical and energetic transmission from the teacher to the student.... The initiations are an ancient formula. The keys to these formulas lie in Reiki symbols. The attunements are a combination of these formulas as well as the teachers' lineage and ability" (Ellyard 2004, 31). In this process, energetic transfers are passed from the teacher to the student thereby aligning the student with what is called, "Universal Energy." According to Stein (1995), the teacher stands behind the student and draws a Reiki symbol. He or she moves in front of the student, repeats the gesture, and then returns behind the student. Both teacher and student generally experience varying phenomena. "Some perceive colors, other see pictures, some experience past lives.... Some are filled with light or a feeling of total peace, wonder or love...." (17).

Following this experience, the students are shown illustrations of twelve hand positions that are used on the body to administer Reiki energy to others. These hand positions line up with the alleged chakras, a Hindu term for energy centers that are located throughout the body and are correlated to various vital organs. Students are given another attunement followed by self-practice for about an hour. Petter (1997, 39) notes, "Even after the first initiation, the feeling of energy flowing through your hands is surprisingly strong and incontrovertible." A third initiation takes place, and students pair up and practice an entire session replete with hand positions. This is followed by a fourth and final initiation. Students are given a level one certificate and asked to undergo a twenty-one day purification period in which they practice Reiki on themselves, drink plenty of water, and abstain from heavy drinking and drugs, However, this purification period is not attached to any type of moral code. It is interesting to note that another term for this period is called "integration."

It is during the twenty-one day purification period that some participants experience "various aches and pains, headaches, nausea, dizzy spells, loose or regular bowel movements and even feel ungrounded.... Some people may experience emotional release in the form of mood swings.... Some people have fits of laughter or get the 'Reiki Giggles'" (Ellyard, 34–35). Whatever manifests is deemed as an essential component of the body's need to eliminate toxins. At the close of the level one initiation process, the participant is permanently connected to Universal energy and can heal self and others as a Reiki channel. It should be noted that the ability to "heal" is believed to have existed within each participant. Reiki has simply served as a catalyst. What is interesting to note is that although each level is designed to "open" you up to greater levels of power, Bearheart, a self-described "escaped" Episcopalian—turned shaman related to me her early experiences of Reiki after being attuned to level one in which she was able to perform distance or absentee healing. Generally, distance healing is taught at level two. She reflected:

> *A friend of mine called me with the diagnosis of cervical cancer. And I hadn't taken the level two Reiki yet. I didn't know how to send it to her house. And I ran upstairs and put my hands on a pillow and talked to God and said, 'You know, I don't know what you're going to do and you'll do whatever is appropriate. My preference, for whatever that may count, is that she live to be an old person and healthy.' And so I put my hands on the pillow approximately where, if it were her torso, where her reproductive system was and my hands got hot and a few moments later I found myself stand—[standing outside of her friend's home]. You want to call this astral projection? I have no idea. Maybe I was just given a vision—standing across the street from her home, looking at iridescent lights going up and down just as though a huge crystal had been fitted over her house—all these sort of soap bubble colors running up and down. And with the few visions that I've had they've all been—and others have supported this—as soon as you realize that you're having it, it's finished....Then I'm back here, my hands are cooling off and I said, 'Okay, I hope something good got to you.' She called me up a couple of days later and said, 'I've had another biopsy, false alarm.' There was a misdiagnosis; they could find no evidence of cancer.*

Level Two

In level two, the knowledge base and power of Reiki is increased. Another attunement takes place, and students are taught how to use three of the four esoteric Reiki symbols believed to intensify the flow of energy. Learning the symbols has the goal of helping the practitioners to connect with the conscious and subconscious mind and to heal emotions. This is in addition to healing the physical body that takes place on level one. Practitioners also learn how to do absentee healing in which the recipient is at a distance. The level also addresses recipients' emotional and mental problems as well as "addictions...[and] planetary issues" (Sunde, 1998). Practitioners are able to apply Reiki to plants, pets, and any situation that could benefit from Reiki energy. In recalling her experience at level two, Bearheart commented, "I'm sure you know there are symbols that are used in level two. There is a mantra or a name that goes with each one which serves as a trigger—Uh, speaking the name of the symbol ritually calls into the room—calls into your presence the ability to communicate. When you say a particular word it translates as 'Put the power here' and then you'll notice that the energy flow has increased." Normally the practitioner "scans" the individual's [energy] field and [in a full session] the hand positions known as mudras are performed over the entire body. Bearheart posited, "If there was... a disturbance there in the body underneath where my hand was—my hand feels either hot or it feels like ginger ale bubbles.... When something is active and saying, 'Please pay attention to me,' ... there's a huge demand [and] your hand gets very hot."

Level Three

The third level is known as the Master level. Different schools often have the level two Reiki practitioners go through several years of apprenticeship under the tutelage of a seasoned Reiki Master before granting level three status. The level is for students who have dedicated their lives to the practice and advancement of Reiki—they are answering the "call." Thus, the practitioner is able to teach and initiate others into levels one and two. They also learn practical skills, such as workshop presentation, group dynamics, and related "spiritual disciplines." More knowledge is passed on through additional attunements, and students are educated about the "master" symbol. Petter (1997) offers, "There is little to be said about the Third Reiki Degree, except that the Master symbol consciously connects us to the divine spark. Some people call it the 'higher self.'" (47). Some schools teach a fourth level in which the Reiki Master can initiate practitioners into all three levels.

Going with the Flow

As mentioned, there are actually two discernable actors in Reiki. While the first is the practitioner, the second is the recipient. In a "typical" full Reiki session, a recipient makes arrangements to meet with a practitioner. Often recipients may complain about a chronic problem, such as back pain; they may be experiencing anxiety or stress; they may be struggling with depression or a host of emotional problems. The goal is to find relief.

The setting is designed to be relaxing and appealing. Thus, there may be a room filled with lit candles, burning incense, or soft music playing in the background. The ideal setup for giving a full Reiki treatment is a room with a massage table. Normally, conversation takes place between the practitioner and the recipient to establish rapport and highlight issues. The practitioner is generally compassionate and attentive. However, there is minimal discussion during the Reiki session. It is not unusual for recipients to fall asleep while Reiki is being administered.

At the start of the session, practitioners have recipients lie flat or their backs. The recipient remains fully clothed. A square folded cloth or hands may be placed over the recipients' eyes to help them to relax. Next, starting at the head of the recipient, practitioners place their hands over twelve different areas of the body that again line up with the invisible chakras. In each position, practitioners place their hands over a particular area of the body for three to five minutes. There are four head, front, and back positions. The number of hand positions varies depending on the school. It is believed that Reiki energy enters through the seventh, or crown, chakra located at the top of the head and the fourth, or heart, chakra located near the center of the chest. However, treatment commences with the sixth, or brow, chakra located between the eyebrows. This particular chakra is influenced by the practitioner's mental repetition of the mantra "Om" (Sunde, 1998). The brow chakra is also known as the third eye where "self awareness, wisdom, higher consciousness, clairvoyance, simple knowing, visualization and conceptual thinking…" emanate (Lubeck, Petter, and Rand, 2001, 86). Ellyard (2004) noted the following sensations felt by the practitioner while scanning the body of the recipient. They included:

> *heat or warmth in the hands, tingling or pulsing up and down the arms and within the body, cold or cool energy, cessation of mental chatter and increased calm, deep relaxation, visual impressions, seeing colors, lights, or images, hands feeling drawn to an area, hands feeling repelled from an area, hands feeling like they are stuck or glued in an area, hands feelings like they are a few inches inside the area that is being worked on, an occasional sharp or dull pain in your hands or arms, a slight vibration in the hands or arms, an increased desire to yawn. (42)*

Many recipients talk about feeling the sensation of heat, tingling, warmth, or cold in various parts of their body. Many fall asleep and awake feeling refreshed. Some reveal that after a session, they feel light-headed and spaced out. For some, it is the feeling of an altered state that may last for several days. There are recipients who have emotional reactions of tears, joy, or agitation. It varies, but many initially feel relaxed. Sometimes, practitioners will discuss insight or images they received as they worked. While many may find Reiki initially brings relaxation and a reduced sensation of pain, these results were not the goals of its founder, Mikao Usui.

Reiki Roots 3

The Legacy of Dr. Mikao Usui and Buddhist Enlightenment

Allegedly, Reiki was "rediscovered" by Dr. Mikao Usui, a Japanese *Christian*, who was both a theologian and a minister. The legend told was that he served as the head of a Christian School, comparable to a seminary in the U.S., in Kyoto, Japan. He was asked by his students to show how Jesus was able to do healing in the Bible. His inability to give a direct answer led him on a journey that ended in a Buddhist monastery.

In speaking with the monks, he discovered that Gautama Buddha had also healed the sick on several occasions through the laying-on of hands. Based on this information, he began to study the Sanskrit sutras (holy writings). There he discovered ancient Tibetan Buddhist healing symbols, but he could not find anything that spoke of how to apply the symbols. This new information led him on a twenty-one day journey up Mount Kurama, a sacred mountain north of Korea, where he fasted and prayed. This contemplative process culminated in a mystical experience that Epperly (2001, 6) noted "not only confirmed the healing power of the ancient symbols he had been studying but also gave him a technique for their use in physical and spiritual healing." In his mystical experience, Usui saw a beam of white light that struck him in the middle of his forehead and knocked him to the ground. While on the ground unconscious, he envisioned millions of rainbow-colored bubbles with Sanskrit symbols inside. According to Kelly (2000) in her book entitled, *Reiki and the Healing Buddha*, this phenomenon mirrored a "description of the Buddhist state of 'Enlightenment.' A similar description was found in the story of Sakyamuni Buddha when he gained 'Enlightenment' under the Bodhi tree" (160). She further asserted:

> This experience which Mikao Usui went through is a description of the 4th degree of Reiki; unknown within the present Reiki system. It is the step which leads to Buddhahood or total oneness with the cosmic energies of the universe. For Mikao Usui, this would have meant complete oneness with the Healing Buddha (the healing energy of the universe) enabling him to become a Master of Healing. (160)

Immediately following this experience, he performed several miracles and ultimately set up a healing clinic in an impoverished area in Japan for seven years. When he discovered that many of the same people that had received physical healing were returning with unchanged lives, he added five principles to the Reiki system that individuals were encouraged to follow. Strangely enough, these five principles had a close correlation to Buddhism and the five meditations or healing Buddhas.

The latest research on Reiki has indicated that aspects of the story just recounted about Dr. Usui were more legendary than factual. Lubeck, Petter, and Rand (2001) in *The Spirit of Reiki* maintained that Hawayo Takata, the Reiki Master who was responsible for bringing Reiki to the West, added "mythological elements" to her retelling of the Reiki story. Records from the Usui Reiki Ryoho Gakkai, the Reiki organization started by Dr. Usui, indicated, "Dr Usui had never been a Christian; he was a Buddhist. Dr. Usui is buried at Saijoji temple, a (Pure Land) Buddhist temple. If he had been a Christian, he would have been buried at a Christian cemetery" (28). Rand maintained that Usui was initially a successful businessman who became a Buddhist monk later in life when his business deteriorated. Furthermore, archived records indicated that Usui was never a faculty member, student, or president at Doshisha University; he did not receive a degree in theology from the University of Chicago. While some have posited that perhaps Dr. Usui assumed an alias thereby preventing historical verification, that assumption was dismissed as speculation since the name "Usui" appeared at his gravesite. The name "Gyoho" was found on his memorial stone, but that name was strictly for use in the afterlife. One other unverifiable statement made by Hawayo Takata was that the formula for Reiki was found in a Buddhist sutra; however, no one could locate this particular sutra. Rand pointed out that by Dr. Ususi's own admission in his handbook *Reiki Ryoho Hikkei*, "Our Reiki Ryoho is something absolutely original and cannot be compared with any other [spiritual] path in the world"(29). He later stated, "First of all, our Reiki Ryoho is an original therapy, which is built upon the spiritual power of the universe" (Lubeck, Petter, and Rand, 29). The authors emphasized:

> Inscribed on the Usui memorial stone it says that the system of Reiki came from Dr. Usui's mystical experience on Mt. Kurama. ...From this we can conclude that Dr. Usui did not rediscover Reiki, but that it is an original form of healing that he developed. Of course, the energy of Reiki may have been part of one or more healing systems previously practiced. However, it appears that Dr. Usui had a powerful mystical experience on Mt. Kurama which he received healing energy directly from the source. (29–30)

Rand, in recollecting Usui's early years, revealed that the young Usui studied kiko, a practice similar to Qi Gong; both practices were designed to stimulate the use of life energy [Ki] and promote hands-on-healing. "The young Usui wondered if a way existed to heal without having to first store up healing energy and then leaving one depleted at the end.... Because of his [Usui's] enhanced *psychic* abilities, he was able to join a metaphysical group called the

Rei Jyutu Ka, where his education about the spiritual world continued" (Lubeck, Petter, and Rand, 13–14).

Reiki's Founder Mikao Usui: Disciple of the Buddha

It is now common knowledge that Usui was a Buddhist; however, not much attention is given to the spiritual disciplines that influenced the unveiling of Reiki. In examining Buddhism, it was a religion that promoted a system of healing, which denied the existence or power of a triune God. The Dharma (the very words of Buddha which represented the "path of awakening") was what the Buddha preached and by his own admission, he was the Supreme Physician without peer. It was the Dharma which brought about healing and salvation to all. Buddha was passionate about the teaching of the Dharma. He preached it, and he praised his followers for teaching it.

It is noteworthy that Buddhist teacher and Reiki Master David F. Vennells, in his recent book *Reiki Mastery*, posited, "The origins of the Usui-Do system are now known to be from Taoism (to be discussed later) brought to Japan from China, probably around the 5th century" (21). Nevertheless, he was quick to assert that while "Dr. Usui taught Reiki to his students from the framework of Buddhism …there were many Masters today who teach Reiki within the framework of…other religions" (9). Halverson (1996) aptly observed that Buddhism had the "ability to assimilate itself into a culture and to influence that culture's underlying beliefs" (54).

According to Miles and True (2003), in terms of spiritual affiliation, Mikao Usui was a "life-long practitioner of Tendai Buddhism and dedicated spiritual aspirant [who] formulated the roots of what has come to be called Reiki in early 20th century Japan" (63). Moreover, in the article, "Pamela Miles, Reiki Vibrational Healing," Miles (2003) in an interview with Bonnie Horrigan offered, "When people came to Usui, he would place his hands on them briefly, giving them a healing, and teach them spiritual practices" (78).

This fact was confirmed by Lawrence Ellyard (2004) in his book, *Reiki Healer*, where sources indicated that "Usui took formal training in Shingon (a sect of esoteric Japanese Buddhism which involves the use of mantras, mudras, and mandalas leading to enlightenment.) He [was] also believed to have undertaken the position of a lay Buddhist Tendai priest (Zaike)" (4). Furthermore, he had the Buddhist name of Gyoho (5). Although there was a paucity of information to substantiate a lifetime practice of Tendai Buddhism, again there was consensus that Mikao Usui was buried in a Pureland Buddhist Saihoji Temple in Tokyo (Ellyard, Stiene, and Rand) thereby supporting his Buddhist faith. Ellyard added that Usui spent a great deal of time collecting and studying Buddhist scriptures, especially Buddhist healing techniques, and he became an advanced practitioner of meditation. A man of versatility, Usui was also well versed in psychology, Taoism, divination, incantations, and physiognomy. Ellyard noted, "Over time, Usui became a respected and learned Buddhist teacher with a following of devoted students.... The focus of his teaching was on healing" (5). It should be understood that the healing emphasized by Usui was spiritual in nature. It was the teaching of the words of Buddha, which set students on the Eightfold Path to enlightenment.

As a Tendai Buddhist priest, Usui would have subscribed to the teachings of the Dharma and taught them, more specifically, the Lotus Sutra. Lai (1987), in "Why the Lotus Sutra? On the Historic Significance of Tendai" found in the *Japanese Journal of Religious Studies*, emphasized:

> Like the Bible to the Christians, the truth of the Lotus is self-evident. This is the Word of the Buddha that declares itself the Eternal Logos.... This is the good news, the preaching of which, like in Pauline evangelical theology resuscitates, re-actualizes, and makes present anew every time the Word of the Buddha and the Logos-Dharma that is the Buddha himself. (84)

According to Hazama Jiko (1987) in "The Characteristics of Japanese Tendai," characteristically speaking, Tendai Buddhism combined the teachings of the Tien-t'ai School, which emphasized the Lotus Sutra and "esoteric Buddhism [referring] to the tantric tradition also represented by the Shingon [S]chool" (103). What is significant and perhaps indirectly responsible for depositing the seeds for some of the practices used in Usui's execution of Reiki is Jiko's description of the precepts taught in esoteric Buddhism and the T'ien-t'ai practice. He noted:

> Esoteric Buddhism teaches the achievement of integration with the Buddha and all aspects of existence, symbolized by the six elements and four types of mandalas, through verbal intonation of mantras, physical performance of mudras [hand positions] and mental concentration.... T'ien-t'ai practice, is not concerned with performing formulaic ceremonies, but seeks contemplative wisdom and insight into the true aspects of reality in a single thought through simple sitting in meditation or contemplation. The later Shingon practice, utilizes various devices and ceremonial activities, the performance of numerous mudras with one's hands and the intonation of mantras, or the contemplation of a wide variety of phenomena, to awaken a realization of or integration with the Dharma body of Buddha.... Tendai claims that the Buddhas which represent these two teachings, Sakyamuni and Vairocana, are one and the same... [that] the Tendai Lotus teaching and Shingon esotericism are in fundamental agreement. (104)

The purpose of the above-mentioned practices was enlightenment, the time when "the body, speech, and mind of man were merged with the body, speech, and mind of the Buddha" (Reverends Jikai and Jiho 2000, 2). Some of the practices, such as mudras, and mantras, were used in past and *current* Reiki practice. While mudras were typically defined as hand positions or gestures used in Reiki, they were also used in "signifying a particular aspect of dharma, also... dance postures and positions of the whole body" Ellyard, 190). Michael Saso (1987) confirmed that utilization of these rituals, also called *upaya*, was viewed as "convenient skillful means to obtain enlightenment" (239).

Stiene and Stiene (2003) noted that Usui made use of mantras also known in Japan as *jumons* or *kotodamas*. They indicated, "The terms *kotodama* and *jumon* accentuate a slightly different aspect of working with sound" (80). While *kotodama* was defined as "words carrying spirit," *jumon* carried the notion of "sound invoking a specific energetic vibration" or a "spell or incantation." This was in keeping with Peter Masefield's research on sound as it related to the recitation of the Dharma. Both terms were also connected to ancient Buddhist Shinto (native religion of Japan) practices (57).

Mantras were given by Usui to his students to facilitate accessing different aspects of energy (59). Hand positions, also known as *mudras*, "were taught [by Usui] to those who found working intuitively difficult. Symbols were also added to the mantra recitations as a helpful tool to evoke specific energy" (59). The fact that symbols and mantras were used in Reiki attunements to create higher levels of vibration and to facilitate the practitioners' ability to channel the energy was confirmed by Nield-Anderson and Ameling (2000) in "The Empowering Nature of Reiki as a Complementary Therapy" (25).

Meditation was also a part of Usui's instruction. However, what distinguished Usui's Reiki from other hands-on-healing methods was his use of *reiju* or *attunements*—currently used in Reiki. Reiju apparently had roots in Tendai Buddhism and "mirrors a Tendai ritual called *go shimbo* also known as Dharma for Protecting the Body" (99).

Fabio Rambelli (2002) in "The Ritual World of Buddhist Shinto" further described Buddhist initiation rituals that were specifically designed to transmit secret knowledge. In his article, he spoke about the "role of Reiki *kanjo* [an initiation ritual]…and the secret initiation to the *Reikiki*, an influential but elusive key text of premodern combinatory religion…[which] after the Meiji Period… was dismissed as syncretic aberrations from "pure" Buddhist… orthodoxy …and have not been studied in depth" (265). Rambelli expounded on how *kanjo* "was a typical esoteric ceremony that served to transmit doctrines and practices and sanctioned the practitioners' level of attainment." It is worth noting that information gained in the initiation rituals carried a "soteriologic goal since it was equivalent to the attainment of salvation (becoming a Buddha...or identifying with one's *kami*" [italics added] (266). "The kami is interpreted here as a life force inside human beings" (273). Most likely, "life force" would refer to Chi or *Ki*, believed to animate humans. The Shinto rituals mirrored those practiced in Tendai temples (267). In these initiations, "the master transmit[ted] to a disciple the essence of esoteric Buddhism" (268).

While the initiation rituals had several components, a practice which reflected current Reiki attunements was when "the master teaches [the student] a mantra and a mudra" (268). The point to be emphasized was that Usui was a Tendai Buddhist who performed some of these practices on his students. While Shintoism represented the indigenous religion of Japan, Rambelli observed, "In his *Jindaikan* shikenmon [a text] Tendai priest Ryohen (late fourteenth to early fifteenth centuries) wrote: 'what Shingon calls *kanjo*, Shinto calls *reiki*; reiki is thus a different term for kanjo [initiation ritual]'" (275). Remember, the Tendai Buddhism Usui practiced was a combination of Shingon [a form of esoteric Japanese Buddhism that promoted Buddhahood through the practice of rituals] and T'ien-t'ai practice. While in the aforementioned initiation rituals, there was no mention of physical healing mediated through the laying-on of hands, it is evident that the *transmission of the Dharma*, the "King of Medicines," was an objective. This fact has been demonstrated in the lives of some of Usui's students.

Prior to Usui's rediscovery of Reiki, his goal was to give students the tools to become *enlightened* and obtain Buddhahood. Hence, the initial healing Usui propagated focused primarily on *spiritual healing*, which resulted from the teaching of the Dharma, the "King of Medicines." In agreement, the Stienes posited, "The aim of Usui's teaching was to provide a method for students to achieve enlightenment....Though enlightenment was the aim, the [physical] healing that was taking place [through Reiki] was a wonderful 'side-effect'" (58). In the administering of *reju* or *attunements* mediated through the laying-on of hands, Usui was "remind[ing] students of their spiritual connection" (57) Hence, Usui utilized the laying-on of hands for healing and a type of spiritual transference as evidenced by him giving attunements.

By his own admission, in Frank Arjava Petter's (1999) biographical sketch, *Reiki The Legacy of Dr. Usui*, Petter translated original documents written by Usui. Usui acknowledged in an interview that Reiki Ryoho was "built upon the spiritual power of the universe...." He maintained that, "we need improvements and restructuring in our lives so we can free our fellow human beings from illness and emotional suffering..." and concluded, "the mind and body are one..." (13-14). When asked if Reiki was a *shinrei ryoho,* a psychic or spiritual form of healing, Usui agreed that it was (15). He noted that "chronic diseases were not as easy to treat..."; however, "all diseases, whether they have been caused by psychological, or physical factors can be healed with Usui Reiki.... It not only heals disease of the physical body, it can also heal bad habits and psychological disorders..." (16). Usui added that "with Reiki energy, the spirit becomes similar to God or Buddha, and we develop the goal of healing our fellow beings... this (through the Buddha similarity) is how we make ourselves and others happy" (16). The mentioning of "God" seemed inconsistent given the primary focus on Buddha; thus, it could have been added in the translation. When asked how Reiki was able to heal, Usui indicated that he did not personally obtain Reiki energy through an initiation ceremony. "While I fasted [and meditated for 21 days] I touched an intense energy and in a mysterious manner, I was inspired... I had been given the spiritual art of healing..." (16). In concluding his interview, Usui offered, "Reiki is a spiritual method that goes beyond medical science. It is therefore not based upon it..." (17). However, he maintained that eventually there would be a convergence between Reiki and science.

Usui believed, "All beings into whom life has been breathed have received as a gift the spiritual ability to heal. The same applies to plants, animals, fish, and insects. But human beings, who represent the culmination point of creation, have the greatest power" (19). Giving plants, animals, and insects the "spiritual ability to heal" blurred the distinctions between humans and other life forms. However, it was very much in keeping with Buddhist thought, which viewed all forms of life as sacred.

Summary: Connecting the Dots

It is evident that Usui was a devout Tendai Buddhist with an intense interest in healing and teaching. Prior to his re-discovery of Reiki, his goal in teaching was Buddhist enlightenment, which indicated spiritual healing of the mind and the possibility of becoming one with the Buddha. As a Tendai Buddhist, this process would have required a teaching of the Dharma—specifically the Lotus Sutra, in addition to other aspects of esoteric Buddhism, meditation, Buddhist precepts, and Pureland teachings (Stiene and Stiene, 59).

It cannot be assumed that all of Usui's teachings were spiritual in nature; however, the literature suggests that spiritual teaching was a primary focus. Moreover, while the practice of Reiki did provide some physical healing, Reiki was spiritual in nature and intended as a spiritual practice. According to an inscription on a memorial stone erected in Usui's honor, it was during a period of extended fasting and meditation that the meditative practice of *Kushu Shinren* was suggested (Ellyard, 4) that "a great energy appeared over his head." This "great energy" that appeared over his head was very similar to the experience that Buddha had when he became "enlightened" and founded the religion of Buddhism. Given its spiritual nature, Usui's students were initiated into the practice of Reiki through attunements, and Usui continued to have a following of students who came for his spiritual teachings in addition to Reiki.

Because recent research unveiled Usui's Buddhist background, most current adherents of Reiki have maintained that practitioners did not have to subscribe to a Buddhist worldview. Furthermore, recipients have been told that Reiki did not conflict with any religious beliefs. However, honest critique would lead to Usui's conclusion that Reiki "was a spiritual system," thus Reiki could not be perceived as a spiritually neutral process (Ellyard, 79). In its early inception in Japan, it was presented to a culture that practiced Buddhism, Shintoism, Confucism, and Taoism—spiritual paths rooted in pantheism and monism. In its *initial* presentation to western culture as a Christian practice, not having to be a Buddhist (although Reiki is seeped in Buddhist practices) to practice or receive Reiki appeared very inclusive. However, "Buddhism has the ability to assimilate itself into a culture and to influence that culture's underlying beliefs" (Halverson, 54). This is significant in that it is indisputable that Reiki has ties to Buddhism in addition to the other pantheistic and monistic religions mentioned. Moreover, there is support in the literature to suggest "Reiki therapy is a healing method based on ancient Buddhist scriptures" (Whelan and Wishnia 2003, 210).

While it is evident that Usui seemed deeply concerned about those in physical or emotional pain around him, it would be naïve to ignore the fact that Usui was a Buddhist. However many Reiki practitioners have done that.

Lauded as a teacher, Usui's primary objective in teaching was the Buddhist goal of enlightenment. In Buddhist thought, he certainly possessed the characteristics of a *Bodisattvas*, one "who has obtained enlightenment, but refuse[d] to enter nirvana in order to guide the unenlightened...." Hence, on earth, "They work[ed] to relieve suffering and guide others down the path of salvation" (Lardie, s.v. "bodisattvas").

While there is no evidence to support that all who Usui healed commenced on the Buddhist path, the literature has clearly demonstrated that some of the esoteric Buddhist practices—practices specifically tied to achieving enlightenment, such as mantras, mudras, and mandalas—were some of the same practices taught and utilized in Usui's Reiki. In concluding this section regarding Mikao Usui, the laying-on of hands was used for two specific purposes, (1) healing using Reiki energy and (2) attunements used in Reiki initiations, which had the power to transmit the teachings of the Dharma. The laying-on of hands identified the recipient of Reiki while the transference of "power" was the spiritual energy known as Reiki.

Before leaving this discussion on Dr. Usui, the question that begs explanation is, "Why did Hawayo Takata 'Americanize' her retelling of the Reiki story?" The authors speculated that Hawayo Takata, a resident of Hawaii, imported Reiki to the West at a time when World War II commenced and the Japanese bombed Pearl Harbor. There was a high level of mistrust directed toward the Japanese, and she perhaps felt that Reiki would be dismissed if it appeared to have Japanese cultural ties. Kelley (2000) offered additional speculation as to why Takakta may have embellished the Reiki story:

> It is believed that Mrs. Takata had added the Christian aspect to the Reiki story so Reiki would be more appealing to Christians in the USA.... I believe that the addition of the much disputed Christian segment to the Reiki story was skillfully done, not just to make it easier to teach Reiki to Christians but to act as a Rosetta stone to enable Christians to interpret the Reiki story. (147, 149)

Since many have believed a Christian initiated this practice, many christianized westerners have been uncritical in their assessment of the healing power behind Reiki, despite the obvious ties to Buddhism and the occult. A discussion about Reiki's founder would be incomplete if there was no examination of the source of the energy used in Reiki.

Tracing Reiki Energy Origins   4

One of the major challenges in discussing Reiki is the lack of scholarly research available specifically dealing with the topic. However, in a close examination of the literature (journals) and "sacred texts," which discuss the energy used in Reiki, the origin of the energy, the healing method of the Buddha, and the spiritual background of Mikao Usui, a much deeper level of insight has been gained.

Miles and True agreed that Reiki, which was considered energy medicine, was also classified as a Biofield Therapy. Concerning Biofield Therapy, they added, "Biofield modalities are defined as those therapies intended to affect energy fields that purportedly surround and interpenetrate the human body.... These therapies which included Reiki... and Therapeutic Touch, involve touch or placement of the hands through biofields, the existence of which have not yet been scientifically proven" (62). They recognized the special challenge involved in researching Reiki since the "subtle energy" could not be measured by current scientific technology. Moreover, they insisted that the "healing traditions" that predated the Western model of medicine be examined. Hence, this led to investigating Reiki's energy known as *Ki*.

Elliot Miller (1992, 26) maintained that bioenergetic medicine like Reiki "resisted the scrutiny of hard science." However, he emphasized the extensive research of parapsychologist Thelma

Moss. Moss scrutinized "healing energies" in various indigenous cultures and found similarities between the Hindu's *prana*, the Hawaiians' *mana*, the Chinese's *Chi*, Hippocrates' 'heat oozing out of my hand,' Mesmer's 'animal magnetism,' and Quimby's 'mind force' (26). Miller noted, "Whenever it has appeared—in ancient paganism, modern occultism, or parapsychological research, this 'life force' has been accompanied by altered states of consciousness, psychic phenomena, and contact with spirits" (26).

While Miles and True acknowledged that *Ki* energy was similar to the Chinese energy, *Chi*, they offered, "It should be noted that the vibration accessed in Reiki arises from non-dual primordial *Chi*... as distinguished from the bioenergetic level of *Chi* stimulated by therapeutic acupuncture" (63). This distinction was helpful in locating the origin of the energy used in Reiki.

Sung Ok Chang (2001), professor and nurse practitioner, noted that the term *Ki*, which was also used in Korea, was "closely related to *Chi* or *Qi* in China and Taiwan, *Ki* in Japan,... and bioenergy in the West. *Chi* or *Qi*, literally meaning vapor, gas, ether, and so forth, had been used in ancient China to denote the vital breath or energy animating the cosmos" (75) She commented that Taoist beliefs attributed disease and poor health to depleted *Ki*.

Traditional Chinese Medicine

While Mikao Usui, a devout Tendai Buddhist, is credited with rediscovering Reiki, the *Ki* mentioned in Reiki ultimately had close ties to the energy spoken about in Traditional Chinese Medicine (TCM). James Miller (2001, n.p.) in "Envisioning the Daoist Body in the Economy of Cosmic Power" stated:

> In traditional Chinese medicine, the human body is viewed first and foremost as a network of systems of energetic transpiration or Qi. Each system of transpiration is an "organ" of which there are two Kinds: *yin* systems (zang) and *yang* systems (fu). The *yin* systems (zang) store the potential energy to maintain the dynamic homeostasis of the body,

and the yang systems (fu) transmit this energy. In the system of traditional Chinese medicine, therefore, the basic physiological principle is the continuous exchange of vital energy according to the pattern of *yin* and *yang*. Since the time of the Book of Changes (Yi Ching), [a book based in divination] this pattern of *yin* and *yang* has been regarded as the basic pattern of the cosmos.

O'Mathuna (2001), in his research on human energy fields therapies, noted that it was believed that *Chi* or *Qi* was the life force that permeated everything, and disease resulted when *Chi/Qi* was disrupted or out of balance. Thus, the goal of Chinese medicine, like Reiki, was to restore the balance of *Chi/Qi* in the body. He stressed how segments of Chinese medicine were exported to Japan around 500 A.D. and how the life force energy in Japan was known as *Ki* (41). While life force energy appeared to be a salient feature in the healing methods of indigenous cultures, a written record of the energy was found in Chinese literature.

The Yellow Emperor's Classic on Medicine/The Nei Ching

Donald Mainfort (2004) in "The Physician-Shaman: Early Origins of Traditional Chinese Medicine" maintained that the most essential text for any historical study of Chinese medicine was found in *The Inner Canon of the Yellow Emperor* commonly known as the *Nei Ching*. He stressed, "The title and premise of the Inner Canon assert a direct connection to the occult medical wisdom born at the dawn of Chinese civilization" (36). He noted that the title, "Yellow Emperor" was "misleading" because an emperor did not write the text (36). Allegedly, the *Nei Ching* was written during the mythological life of Emperor Hung Ti from 2697 to 2599 B.C. and was the conversations which took place between "Hung Ti and his minister/physician Chi Po" about various diseases and illnesses (Reisser, Mabe, and Verlarde, 92). History dates the text at 300 B. C. (Chan, 2001). The Yellow Emperor was thought to be the China's first ancestor, and the concept of the energy known *as Ki*,

Chi, or *Qi* (used interchangeably) was first written about in one of the Chinese documents he allegedly authored. "*The Inner Canon of the Yellow Emperor* regard[ed] diseases as an imbalance of 'Qi,' or 'vital air' in the blood vessels and prescribes treatments for healing the imbalances" (Mainfort, 36). In referencing the *Nei Ching*, James Miller commented:

> ...The Yellow Emperor spoke: [The two categories] *yin* and *yang* are the underlying principle of heaven and earth; they are the web that holds all ten thousand things secure; they are father and mother to all transformations and alterations; they are the source and beginning of all creating and killing; they are the palace of spirit brilliance. In order to treat illnesses one must penetrate to their source [which is Chi energy]. (Miller, n.p.)

In Zhu Ming's (2001) verbatim translation of *The Medical Classic of the Yellow Emperor*, he commented, "The philosophers of ancient times regarded that the source of the cosmos was the 'essential *Qi*,' and that everything in the world was produced by the essential *Qi*. The *Qi* is an invisible materialistic element that forms everything. Humans are endowed with the essential *Qi* from nature, and it is called . . . 'essential *Qi*,' 'vital *Qi*,' or 'original *Qi*.' " (7). One very telling comment was made in the discussion of disease-causing pathogens. In the *Nei Ching*, it was clearly believed that man and nature were intricately interrelated; hence the theoretical/metaphysical moorings of *Qi, yin, yang*, the five elements, and the maintenance of balance of each to prevent disease. In yet another section of the *Nei Ching*, (4.1 Third Article, Discussion of Vital-Qi Corresponding to the Heaven), it was stated by the Emperor:

> From ancient times, people who knew the heavenly law realized that the basis of life is rooted in the yin and yang.... If the heavenly *Qi* is clear, one's mental state will be sound. Obedience to it makes the *yang Qi* secure. Though evils exist,

they cannot poison men. . . . Therefore, sages concentrate their minds, acclimatize themselves to the heavenly *Qi*, and integrate the *Qi* of yin and yang of nature with their own. (117)

The fact that the Emperor intimated that sages could keep evil and indirectly disease be it physical or mental away from them by obedience to the heavenly *yang Qi* and not to a sovereign Creator led Ming to pose the question, "Was the world created by a Supreme Being?" His response brings insight into the mysterious nature of *Qi*. He replied, "No. The *Qi* of the yin and yang of nature produced the five elements…[air, water, earth, metal, wood]. That is to say, the *Qi* of *yin* and *yang* of the cosmos made the world" (117). Ming concluded, "This viewpoint dealt a heavy blow at the prevailing superstitious notions of a Creator" (117). It appeared that the force known as *Qi* took the place of God.

In agreement with Ming's discussion on *Qi*, Maoshing Ni's (1995) translation of *The Yellow Emperor's Classic of Medicine* indicated that "all disorders can be attributed to the blood and *Qi* not arriving at certain streams and valleys and caves, an analogy of [acupressure] points" (43). In another section of the text, it was stressed that, "Many diseases come from disharmony of the *Qi*" (149). Finally, it was stated, "The key to effective medicine is to determine the cause and rectify the imbalance of the *yuan*/original *Qi* of the body" (293). It is noteworthy that Ni asserted, "*The Nei Ching of the Yellow Emperor* is one of the most important classics of Taoism" (12).

Taoism and the Nei Ching

According to Lit-Sen Chang (1999), Chinese scholar, theologian, and apologist, in his work *Asia's Religions: Christianity's Momentous Encounter With Paganism*, Taoism was both a philosophy and religion of China started by Lao Tzu and Chuang Tzu, both contemporaries of Buddha. Additionally, Lit-Sen Chang noted that Taoism "is also the called the teachings" of Huang [Ti, the mystical Yellow Emperor]. He stressed, "Taoism as a philosophy is of a very high order, while Taoism as a religion is a debased form full of superstition and idolatry" (87).

Sir Norman Anderson (1984), in *Christianity and World Religions: The Challenge of Pluralism,* agreed, "Taoism [is] an abstruse philosophy . . . strangely blended with a riot of cosmology, magic and even demonology" (62). An astute observation made was that "traditional Chinese medicine was the Child of Chinese religion. At their core, both share the same ingredients: the Tao, yin and yang, the invisible energy *Chi* [*Qi/Ki*] and the five elements" (Reisser, Mabe and Verlade, 92).

While some have argued that Chinese medicine was based on science and not religion, it was Mainfort's insight on the work of nineteenth century anatomist, Wang Qingren that inadvertently challenged the notion of TCM's foundation being rooted in science. In a book Qingren wrote in 1830 entitled *Revisions of Medicine,* he maintained that air as opposed to blood circulated in the arteries. This air was known as "*Qi*" or "heavenly air" or "ether" and ill health resulted when there were imbalances in the *Qi* (37). Hence, when traditional Chinese medical doctors did pulse diagnosis (the foundation of Chinese medicine's assessment of illness) in 400 B.C., they believed that "what they were analyzing were pulses of *Qi*, not blood" (37). A major problem with the diagnosis, regardless of the accuracy, was that dissection of the human body or animals was prohibited; thus, there was no "scientific" understanding of the human body or the circulatory system. Moreover, Wang unsuccessfully fought to change the prohibition regarding dissection. He argued, "*Healing* without knowledge of internal organs was like 'a blind man stumbling in the dark'" (37).

Perhaps this acknowledgement by Qingren was the reason Mainfort regarded the premise of the *Nei Ching* as "having direct connection to occult medical wisdom" (36). Mainfort observed, "Regardless of empirical findings through trial and error, all "true" medical knowledge was thought to have emanated from the Yellow Emperor in the legendary past" (37). Consequently, theories about how healing took place were tied to a spiritual worldview which believed in the inner-connectedness of all things and was significantly linked to Taoism, the religion propagated by Lao Tzu, whose teachings were allegedly those of mystical Yellow Emperor.

The connection of *Qi/Chi* to the *Nei Ching*, thus connecting it also to Taoism was immensely significant because, in the discussion of the healing energy used in Reiki, often there is a concerted effort to excise the religious moorings of the energy and present it as a purely scientific manifestation. However, the literature has presented strong evidence to confirm the spiritual ties of Reiki energy to Taoism, especially in relationship to the mystical *Qi/Chi* referenced in the *Nei Ching*.

Mainfort noted how physicians/shaman during 400 BCE began to write about a "way" of medicine. "They combined occult family oral traditions . . . with a natural history of the period in which the modern categories of religion, magic, and science are not clearly differentiated. The 'way' of medicine was strongly influenced by [T] Daoist philosophy, principally the 'Yin-Yang' and 'Five Elements' concepts" (36).

Any reference to the [T] Daoist religion/philosophy as it related to the energy known as *Chi, Qi,* or *Ki,* would be incomplete if the literature regarding the source of this energy was not highlighted. In Miles and True's article, it was stressed that the energy assessed in Reiki "[arose] from non-dual primordial *Chi* or *Tao*" (63). This non-dual primordial *Chi/Qi* was emphasized in another highly venerated book of both Classical Taoism and Chinese culture, entitled the *Tao Te Ching*, which was translated as *The Classic of the Way and Virtue*. Another title was the *Taishang xuanyuan Daodejing*, meaning the *Classic of the Way and Virtue of the Highest Primordial Mystery* (Chan, 5). According to Victor H. Mair (1990, "preface"), "Next to the Bible and the [Hindu] *Bhagavad-Gita*, the *Tao Te Ching* is the most widely translated book in the world." He noted that "the Tao, or Way or [Dao], which is at the heart of the *Tao Te Ching*, is also *the centerpiece of all Chinese religion and thought*" (Mair, "preface").

Tao Te Ching

According to Chan (2002), although Lao-tzu was considered the founder of Taoism and the author of the *Tao Te Ching*, current scholarship has challenged his actual existence. Court historian Sima Qian (ca. 145-86 BC.E.) of the Han dynasty gave a biographical account of Lao-Tzu in the *Shiji* (*Records of the Historian*). He was allegedly a native of Chu and had the surname Li. Other names included Er, Dan and *Laozi*, which was translated as "Old Master" (1). On several occasions, he was believed to have given counsel to Confucius concerning funeral rites. Hence, a Confucian work entitled *Liji* (*Record of Rites*) referenced Lao-Tzu four times (2). Sima Qian went on to say, "Laozi cultivated Dao and virtue... his learning was devoted to self effacement and not having fame" (Chan, 2). He lived in Zhou, China, for many years and left after observing its gradual decline. However, before disappearing, he was allegedly asked by Yin Xi, the official who guarded China's border to the outside world, to record some of his thinking. It resulted in the writing of the *Tao Te Ching* (2).

As previously mentioned, because many scholars found the information located in the *Shiji* difficult to document, William G. Boltz (1993) in his essay "Lao [T]zu Tao [T]e [C]hing." concluded, "it [the *Shiji*] contains virtually nothing that is demonstrably factual; we are left no choice but to acknowledge the likely fictional nature of the Lao-Tzu figure"(270). Despite the lack of agreement among scholars, Lao-Tzu and the *Tao Te Ching* are still highly revered in Chinese as well as other cultures.

Chan offered that when the first Daoist (also Taoist) religious movement appeared in the second century, the legendary stories surrounding Lao-Tzu and the *Tao Te Ching* gained greater popularity. "In the eyes of the faithful, the Dao[Tao] is a divine reality, and Laozi is seen as the personification of the Dao.... [Hence]the writing of the [*Tao Te Ching*], which in religious Daoism commands devotion... [is] a foundational scripture that promises not only wisdom but also immortality to those who submit to its power" (3). It is noteworthy that the Daoist system of belief not only affected Chinese, Korean, and Japanese culture but also "had a close interaction . . . [with] Buddhism, and indigenous traditions such as Shinto" (3). During the seventh century, the Tao Te Ching was translated into Sanskrit, the same language of the symbols used in Reiki.

Foundational Commentaries

It is not unusual in the study of writings that are viewed as sacred texts for there to be commentaries which are designed to explain or interpret the meaning of the text. Thus, in understanding aspects of the *Tao Te Ching*, it is helpful to look at some of the initial commentaries used to facilitate interpretation.

Chan pointed out that in attempting to interpret the *Tao Te Ching*, it is essential to understand that as a text, it is "polysemic" (Robinet 1998) or subject to a variety of interpretations. However, there were four early commentaries that greatly influenced current interpretations of the text. The first was the Heshanggong's *Laozi Zhangfu* from the Han period, which some Japanese scholars dated to the sixth century. "The Heshanggong commentary shares with other Han works the cosmological belief that the universe is constituted by Qi or 'vital energy.' On this basis, interpreting the text in terms of yin-yang theory, the [*Tao Te Ching*] is seen to disclose not only the mystery of the origin of the universe but also the secret to personal well-being"(9).

The second commentary was the *Laozi-zhigui* (*The Essential Meaning of the Laozi*) which also "subscribe[d] to the yin-yang cosmological theory . . ." (10). However, the emphasis was not on cultivating *Qi* energy inasmuch as stressing the cultivation of self, which embraced the principals of non-aggressive action *(wuwei)* and naturalness—simply put, allowing 'nature to take its course' (10).

The third commentary, which highlighted the religious import of the *Tao Te Ching*, was *Xiang'ers' Commentary*. Its original text, despite controversy around the date, was traced to 200 C.E. (10). What is most significant about the commentary is that, "it accepts without question the divine status of the *Laozi* [another name for the *Tao Te Ching*]. Xiang'er invites a larger audience to participate in the quest for the Dao, to achieve union with the Dao through spiritual and moral discipline" (10). The union would take place because of "nourishing one's vital *Qi* through meditation..." (10). The end result would be the formation of "a spiritual body devoid of the blemishes of mundane existence (Rao 1991)" (Chan, 10).

A fourth early commentary that waxed more philosophical than religious was Wang Bi's Laozi Commentary. Wang Bi (226–249) was one of the leaders of a group called the "Learning of the Mysteries (Dao)" (11). Wang Bi concerned himself with the order or "logic of creation. Dao constitute[d] the absolute 'beginning' in that all beings have causes and conditions that derive logically from a necessary foundation" (11). Many past and present followers embraced the philosophical interpretations of the *Tao Te Ching*. However, the Heshanggong Commentary promoted the belief that the universe was comprised of *Qi* that dominated Chinese culture. What is most critical is that "the authority of the Heshanggong Commentary can be traced to its place in the Daoist religion, where it ranks second only to the [*Tao Te Ching*] itself" (11). Thus, according to the literature, the vital healing energy known as *Qi /Chi/Ki* cannot be divorced from the Daoist religion or the alleged source/beginning of all things, the mysterious Tao.

5 A Beginning of All Things?

The Mysterious Tao

In Stephen Mitchell's (1988) translation of the *Tao Te Ching*, the following descriptions were given to emphasize the Tao as the origin of all things and to reflect on the Tao's inscrutable nature. He wrote:

> The Tao is called the Great Mother: empty yet inexhaustible, it gives birth to infinite worlds. It is always present within you. You can use it any way you want. (6)
>
> There was something formless and perfect before the universe was born. It was serene. Empty. Solitary. Unchanging. Infinite. Eternally present. It is the mother of the universe. For lack of a better name, I call it the Tao. (Mitchell, chap. 25 and p. 25)
>
> Look, and it can't be seen. Listen, and it can't be heard. Reach, and it can't be grasped. Above, it isn't bright. Below, it isn't dark. Seamless, unnamable, it returns to the realm of nothing. Form that includes all forms, image without an image, subtle, beyond all conception. Approach it and there is no beginning; follow it and there is no end. You can't know it, but you can be it, at ease in your own life. Just realize where you come from: this is the essence of wisdom. (Mitchell, chap. 25 and p. 14)

In the translation of chapters, 25 and 6, the Tao was thought to represent *the source and origin of all things*. Jacob Needleman in Gia-Gu Feng and Jane English's (1989 and 1972, xi) translation of the *Tao Te Ching* pointed out that in chapter 25, "The picture before us is of a cosmic force or principle that expands or flows outward, or more precisely, descends into the creation of the universe, 'the ten thousand things....' Every created entity ultimately is what it is and does what it does owing to its specific reception of the *energy* radiating from the ultimate formless reality."

Mary Evelyn Tucker (1998) in "Religious Dimensions of Confucianism: Cosmology and Cultivation" noted that cosmology embodied "principles of order that support integrated forms of being that explain the origin, production, and transformation of things" (18). "It is in this sense that cosmologies have a religious dimension because they can give spiritual order and moral direction to a person's life" (9). Thus, what resurfaced in the cosmological framework of the Tao was the notion of a *primordial or primitive Chi/Qi or energy, which was earlier referenced by Miles and True as the healing energy assessed in Reiki.*

In Hua-Ching Ni's (1979) translation of the *Tao Te Ching*, found in the *Complete Works of Lao Tzu*, he further elucidated the primitive energy in both chapters 6 and 14. However, the term "Tao" was replaced with "subtle essence." It is noteworthy that the author Hua-Ching Ni had a family background of healing, spirituality, and the practice of TCM. He viewed TCM as "the application of spiritual development" (back of book). His initial translation of the *Tao Te Ching,* while over 25 years old, embodied a mystical flavor similar to ontological moorings of current adherents of energy medicine or Subtle Energy Modalities (SEM). He wrote:

> The subtle essence of the universe is active. It is like an unfailing fountain of life, which flows forever in a vast and profound valley. It is called the Primal Female and the Subtle Origin. The Gate of the Subtle Origin becomes the root of the

universe. It subtly and gently generates without exhausting itself. (Ni, chap. 6 and p.13)

You may call it Form of the Formless or the Image of the Imageless. Yet the elusive, subtle essence remains nameless. If you hope to meet it, it has no place you can call front, it has no place you call behind. Yet it can be observed in the constant regularity of the universe [nature]. The constancy of the universe of antiquity is the constancy of the present time. If one knows the Primal Beginning, one may thus know the truth of the universal subtle Way. (Ni, chap. 14 and p. 22)

While chapter 6 gave the Tao a clearly grounded maternal image, chapter 14 served to demonstrate the transcendence of the Tao. Similar to the healing energy purported in Reiki, the amorphous Tao was not perceived by the senses. "Dao can only be described as "dark" (*xuan*) or *wu*, literally "not having" any form, or other characteristics of things" (Chan 2001, 14). In Mitchell's paradoxical translation of chapter 14 regarding the Tao, he asserted, "You can't know it, but you be it, at ease in your own life" (Mitchell, chap.14. and p. 14).

In Robert G. Hendricks' (1989) translation of the *Tao Te Ching*, he also highlighted the Tao as the origin of the universe and introduced the concept of *Chi*, *Yin* and *Yang*. He wrote:

The Way [Tao] gave birth to the One. The One gave birth to the Two. The Two gave birth to the Three. And the Three gave birth to the ten thousands things. The ten thousand things carry Yin on their backs and wrap their arms around Yang. Through the blending of chi they arrive at a state of harmony. (Hendricks, chap. 42, and p. 106)

Chan noted the difficulty in understanding chapter 42 but offered that the notion of a Creator similar to the god known as Shangdi, (Lord on High) in ancient Chinese religion seemed incongruous with the concept of transcendence (Chan, 14). Thus, he offered:

The dominant interpretation in traditional China is that the Dao represents the source of the original undifferentiated, essential *qi* energy, the "One," which in turn produces the yin and yang cosmic forces. While the yang energy rises to form heaven, yin solidifies to become earth. A further "blending "of the two generates a "harmonious" *qi*-energy that informs human beings. This is essentially the reading of the Heshanggong commentary. Although the *Laozi* may not have entertained a fully developed yin-yang cosmological theory, which took shape during the Han period, it does suggest at one point that natural phenomena are constituted by yin and yang. (ch. 42). That which gave rise to the original *qi*-energy is indescribable. The *Laozi* calls it Dao, or perhaps more appropriately in this context, "the Dao," with the definite article to signal its presence as the source of the created order. In modern terms, minus the language of yin-yang cosmology, this translates into an understanding of the Dao as 'an absolute entity' which is the source of the universe. (Chan, 14–15)

The Tao and the Christian God

Given its creative abilities, some have concluded that the Tao was yet another name for the one whom Christians have called God. This was a critical insight since Christians believed that God was the source of true healing. Physician Kay Keng Khoo (1998), in "The Tao and the Logos: Lao Tzu and the Gospel of John," emphasized Lao Tzu's recognition of the chaos that resulted when individuals strayed from the "One" meaning a turning away from the Tao. She asserted that Lao Tzu was simply ignorant of the fact that "it require[d] the incarnation of the Logos, that is the Tao, to do the redemptive works necessary to restore human beings to perfection, that is, to harmony with the One" (83–84). She concluded, "The doctrine of the Trinity will illumine this redemptive work done in this world by the Tao. Just as Jesus Christ is rightly identified with the Logos, so He is also rightly identified with the Tao" (84). While

A Beginning of All Things? 63

one could envision a curious logic in Khoo's assessment, it is unsubstantiated given the findings in other literature.

Suggesting an opposing view, Judith Berling (1982) in her discussion of the Tao noted, "Classical Taoist philosophy...was a reinterpretation and development of an ancient nameless tradition of nature worship and divination" (1). She emphasized how the alleged authors of the *Tao Te Ching* lived in a time of social unrest and "religious skepticism." Hence, they "developed the notion of the Dao (Tao—way, or path) as the origin of all creation and the force—unknowable in its essence but observable in its manifestation—that lies behind the functioning and changes of the natural world. They saw in [T]ao and nature the basis of a spiritual approach to living" (1). Thus, health in the mind, body, and spirit flourished when one's life was lived in harmony with the Tao.

Jun Ki Chung (1997) in "Taoism in Christian Perspective" acknowledged that the Tao in a variety of ways seemed similar to the Christian God. She observed that both God and the Tao were "absolute, transcendental, and eternal" (2). However, in contrast to Khoo's assessment, she indicated ways in which they were dissimilar. She posited:

> There are great differences, however, between Lao-tzu's Tao and the Christian God. Lao-tzu's Tao ultimately returns to Nature (tzu-jan), which models itself on that which is on its own. The transcendental Tao merges itself with nature, demonstrating that Tao is in Nature. In brief, Tao exists in nature, which is impersonal and not theistic. On the other hand, the Christian God manifested in the Bible is quintessentially personal. This God feels, speaks, and commands. Whereas Tao never requires any kind of [imposed] obedience, the Biblical God demands absolute obedience or kind obedience, the Biblical God demands ... fidelity. While the Tao is not the object of worship, the Christian God is the only sovereign ruler of the heavens and the earth to be worshipped solely. Moreover, Lao-tzu' Tao does not mention

religious rituals and sacrifices, yet the Biblical God accepts religious sacrifices of a contrite heart.... The followers of Tao do not need to present themselves in specific buildings to mediate upon the Tao, but Christians meet regularly in churches. Lao-tzu does not pray to the Tao, while Christians pray to their God. Tao does not have a mediator to save the world, while Christianity had Jesus Christ as God's one and only Son who came to save sinners. (2)

While maintaining that both Christ and Lao-tzu were invested in living a life of peace, she recognized that Lao-tzu bypassed the linear progression of history that chronicled creation, man's fall, his redemption, and the return of Christ. "Lao-tzu accepte[d] the circular notion of history or the cosmic principle of eternal return. In this continual return of history, Lao-tzu does not allow for the hierarchy of 'God-the human-the material world,' which Christianity asserts. For Lao-tzu, the human, animals, and all things belong to one 'category,...'" (4).

Lit-Sen Chang in his critique of both Taoism and the Tao again concluded that religious Taoism was replete with polytheism, demonism, and idolatry. While there was a pantheon of gods in religious Taoism, there existed three main figures. They included the Jade Emperor who was believed to be the Creator, The Precious spirit who served as the "Great Priest," and Lao-tzu who was thought to be a reincarnation of the Jade Emperor (Chang 1999, 89). However, all of these venerated figures were subject to the Tao. Thus, the Jade Emperor, while given the title of creator of heaven and earth, was not seen as the Creator who was the source of all things. It was noted that in philosophical Taoism, the notion of a Creator was believed to be a myth and thus dismissed. Moreover, it was Chang's observation about the Tao in philosophical Taoism that solidified its distinctiveness from Christianity's God. He aptly observed:

> Taoism as a philosophy had, in fact, no God to worship. Taoism of philosophy may be said to be deistic because the

A Beginning of All Things? 65

Tao is nature. It teaches us to know nature, to conform to nature, and not to interfere with nature; instead we are to be subject to nature. It can also be said to be pantheistic because the Tao is all-embracing. One is all, and all is one. Everything has Tao within it.

Tao is the first cause and the creative force of nature and of the universe. It is the essence of all substances and the regulator of all movements. It is the source and support of all things. It is without substance, yet contains within it all substance as the all-producing, all nourishing, and all-perfecting. However, Taoism is destitute of the sense of the real Creator. (89)

According to the literature, *it was from this impersonal model of "ultimate reality" that the energy used in Reiki, "primordial* Chi," *emerged.* This reality was replete with *Qi, yin,* and *yang* and was also known as the Tao or "The Way." In some instances, the "Way" was impersonal and enigmatic. Yet, in other instances, the "Way" seemed to "dictate spiritual order and moral direction" (Tucker 1998, 9). The Tao [Way] "didn't take sides but gave birth to both good and evil" (Mitchell, chap. 5). It encouraged people to "Throw away holiness and wisdom ... and [they] would be a hundred times happier" (Mitchell, chap. 19). The Tao [Way] was detached from all things and desirous of nothing. (Mitchell, chap. 7). Nevertheless, the Tao [Way] according to Stephen Mitchell, [like Reiki], was to be surrendered to. "In surrendering to the Tao [Way], in giving up all concepts, judgments, and desires, [the] mind has grown naturally compassionate..." (xiii).

As a consequence of surrendering to the Tao, humans were better able to love others and see "beyond good and evil" and thus "embody the good. Until finally, [they] are able to say, in all humility, "I [as opposed to Jesus] am the Tao, the Truth, the Life" (ix). Mitchell added, "The teaching of the *Tao Te Ching* was moral in the deepest sense because individuals were "unencumbered by any concept of sin..." (ix). Thus, [one] "doesn't see evil as a force to resist, but simply as an opaqueness, a state of self-absorption which is in disharmony with the universal process…" (ix). Those who were "out of harmony with the universal process" could… "open themselves to the Tao…be at one with the Tao…trust [their] natural responses…and everything would fall into place" (chap. 23).

Implications of Tao as Creator

From the literature, it is evident that the mysterious Tao, presented as the originator of all things, was *dissimilar* to the God of the Bible, Creator of all things and the source of all true healing—the one who sought out a personal relationship with humans through the redemptive work of Jesus. In fact, the notion of having a moral and holy God who served as the Creator was actually perceived as a myth. Fredrick Mote (1971) highlighted a significant and unique aspect of Chinese thought in that many felt that humankind and the world were "uncreated, … and constituting the central features of a spontaneously self-generating cosmos having no creator, god, ultimate cause, or will external to itself" (17-18).

For the Chinese, a greater emphasis was placed on the "continuity of being," a major facet of Taoist thought (Tucker, 9). Because the Tao represented "both the grounding and the growing dimensions of cosmology and cultivation," the concept of a personal God who served as Creator was viewed as a tradition of the West and other monotheistic cultures; hence, two positions arose (16). One was an "emanationist" position and the other was a "creationist" position. Tucker explained, "The major distinction between these two approaches is that the…emanationist position does not presume that there is a cleavage [connection] between the Tao and the world, whereas the creationist position does posit a dualism between God and the world" (16-17).

Because there was no perception of a personal God, the way to health and healing was to live in harmony with an impersonal cosmic force, which was endowed with healing energy accessible to all. This harmony or freedom from sickness and disease resulted when *yin* and *yang* were in perfect balance and the vital primordial *Chi*, which emanated from the Tao, was unobstructed. However, again, if *Chi* was blocked, Reiki practitioners could mediate healing by unblocking and balancing *Chi* or the subtle energies.

The Non-religious Religious Tao

One unsubstantiated claim is that Reiki, as a therapy, was non-religious. However, it has been established through the literature that primordial *Chi* was tied to the *Tao* and the *Tao* was connected to the religion and philosophy of Taoism. While it has been recognized that Reiki practitioners could deny allegiance to either philosophical or religious Taoism, denial does not remove the cosmological beliefs about the foundation of the energy practitioners claimed to access. The Tao was believed to be the origin of the universe. If the Tao was the source of all things, the Tao as a creative force or cosmic energy was also the source of healing; hence, the preoccupation with balancing *Chi* energy, *yin* and *yang*, and living in harmony with the *Tao*. For, it was widely accepted that surrendering to the Tao would ensure personal well-being. In fact, "Yielding to the movement of the Tao in lives would bring inner transformation and eternal peace" (Lardie, s.v. "taoism"). Again, even in cosmological terms, there was the suggestion of religion in that the Tao sought to "dictate moral and spiritual direction."

As previously mentioned, the Tao has also been identified as "The Way." This of course suggests a path that one was encouraged to follow. While on the surface, the commanding language of dogmatic "religion" is not present, the subtle "counsel" found in the *Tao Te Ching* of surrender and non-assertive action (*wuwei*) to an unknowable force is very dominant. What is most striking is the similarity of the Tao to the healing energy of Reiki; there is a significant parallel between the "Way" of the Tao and the "Way" of Reiki energy. Reiki Master Rand offered:

> By treating yourself and others and meditating on the essence of Reiki, you will be guided more and more by Reiki

in making important decisions.... Over time, you will learn from experience that the guidance of Reiki is worth your trust. Once you have surrendered completely, you will have entered the Way of Reiki....

...In the end, we must consider that a Reiki-Master is not one who has mastered Reiki, but one whom Reiki has mastered. This requires that we surrender completely to the spirit of Reiki, allowing it to guide every area of our lives and become the only focus and source of nurturing and sustenance. (1999, n.p.)

In like manner, Miles (2003) in "Reiki Vibrational Healing" recommended:

The more we practice [Reiki], the more the practice gives us. This continues to be true for me as a Reiki master. I haven't mastered Reiki; if anything Reiki has mastered me! The longer I practice, the more I rely on my silent partner. I think of myself as the delivery system [channel] and focus on making my client comfortable and listening deeply while the pulsation of Reiki accomplishes the healing. For years, I thought I was learning to do something. One day I realized I was simply learning how to stay out of the way. The *Tao Te Ching* expresses it beautifully: "When nothing is done, nothing is left undone." (81)

Taoism and Buddhism

Before leaving the discussion on the Tao, it is critical to note that there is a undeniable link between Taoism and Buddhism. Moreover, practitioners of Reiki will *now* admit that historical records indicate that Usui was a Buddhist. Several authors have been able to make the connection.

O'Hyun Park (1975), in *Perspectives in Religious Studies*, noted the inner-connectedness of Confucianism, Taoism, and Buddhism in Chinese culture. He observed, "While Confucianism and Taoism are indigenous crystallizations out of the matrix of Chinese primitivism, Buddhism was an imported religion, but was thoroughly domesticated and suffused with the Chinese spirit. Thus, Buddhism entered China not only as a displacer of what was already in place there but as a partner in an enlarged enterprise" (159). Buddhism was not only imported to China but eventually migrated to Japan as well.

In agreement, Terence C. Russell (1990) in *Taoist Resources* posited, Buddhism has developed along side of the indigenous Daoist religion in a state of interaction and mutual influence. The doctrinal and institutional boundaries of the two religions were at times exceedingly fluid" (54). The veracity of this statement was supported in a text called the *Tozuihen* or the *Peach Blossom Collection*, compiled by Chinese and Buddhist Monks in the eighteenth century. Russell noted that the text "provides us with an interesting case in the history of borrowing and accommodation between Buddhism and Daoism" (54).

Livia Kohn (1993) confirmed the insight of both Park and Russell by reflecting on Taoist and Buddhist scriptures. She offered:

> Many Taoist scriptures were in fact created as close copies of the Buddhist Sutras, when—in the fifth century—the religion was eagerly striving to establish itself as a teaching acceptable to broader segments of this population and at the imperial court. The Taoist religion as a whole developed under the strong influence of Buddhism, not only in it scriptures but also in its doctrines, cosmology, organization, and practices. (51)

It was Park's comments on the spirit of "Chinese religiosity" that best summarized the union between Taoism and Buddhism. He emphasized, "The fundamental *way* of the…religions are similar. The deepest Chinese feeling in the matter is that each…is complete in itself, that each points to the same ultimate goal, that the goal may be reached along the path prescribed by each, but that nonetheless, each is in need of as well as supplementary of the other…" (159).

Summary: Connecting the Dots

In examining the literature that highlighted the origins of Reiki energy known as *Ki*, it necessitated the examination of similarly-named energies, *Qi* and *Chi*, all germane to Asian culture. It was discovered that the theoretical underpinnings of these energies could be traced to Traditional Chinese Medicine and the venerated text, the *Nei Ching* translated as *The Yellow Emperor's Classic on Chinese Medicine*. However, what has been called "primordial" *Chi*, could be traced to the *Tao Te Ching, The Book of the Way and Virtue* and a powerful yet unknowable cosmic force referred to as the Tao or the Way. Other translations of the *Tao Te Ching* referred to the Tao as "Universal Oneness and the Ultimate Reality."

The literature has demonstrated that the Tao, which was "at the heart of the *Tao Te Ching*, [was] also the centerpiece of all Chinese religious thought" (Mair, n.p.). The alleged author and founder of the Taoist religion and philosophy, Lao-Tzu, was believed by many to be a "personification [incarnation] of the Tao," and the Tao was accepted as divine. While Reiki practitioners have vehemently resisted the notion that Reiki energy had any religious or spiritual underpinnings, Reiki adherents have equated the healing energy accessed in Reiki to the same "power or force" used by Jesus Christ. The paradox is that Jesus' spirituality could not be separated from his identity, nor could it be excised from his personal relationship to Father God as Creator and the Holy Spirit. It is evident that the "Way" and path to healing and harmony resulting from surrender to the impersonal Tao or Reiki energy is a worldview that is distinct from a biblical worldview. The question which now begs answering is, "Exactly what is the worldview that is being promoted when Reiki energy is utilized?"

A Pantheistic Worldview   6

Defining Worldview

In looking at Reiki origins found in Taosim and Buddhism, while there are distinctions, there are also similarities which stem from the fact that a worldview is shared. James Eckman (2006) in *The Truth about Worldviews* explains:

> A worldview is the core of what we believe. It answers the basic questions of life. How did we get here (creation and the universe)? Where are we going (the meaning of history)? What is the nature of reality (physical or spiritual or both)? What is the nature of God, or transcendent reality? What is the nature of truth (objective or subjective)? What is the nature of human beings? What happens to human beings when they die? What guidelines determine human behavior (ethics)? (6)

The worldview which supports Reiki is pantheism. In pantheism, the religions of Hinduism, Buddhism, and Taoism are considered. Reality is spiritual. However, Leffel (1994) added, "Eastern pantheists believe spiritual reality is ultimately impersonal and unknowable. Spirit is more like energy than a personal God.... Most of the pantheistic religions involve devotion to a host of gods" (9). What is perceived as material or physical is *maya* or an illusion. God is an "impersonal spiritual reality" known as *Brahman*, the Ultimate reality (10). However, *Brahman* is incapable of being comprehended in a personal manner. Human beings are *monistic* or one with reality, and the human essence is *atman*, again "impersonal, undefinable, spiritual reality" (10). Thus, *atman* and *Brahman* are one in the same because the concept of individual existence is an illusion. Truth is subjective and represents one's connection with the universe, yet there are no words to explain truth. Reasoning or rational thought would never allow one to understand the impersonal, ungraspable *Brahman*. Since individual personhood and reality are rejected, objective values do not exist. In fact, the notion of good or evil is simply an illusion. Therefore, there is no real difference between good and evil. While experience and reason dictate that individuality exists and one's personality is distinct from one's existence, the perception of individuality results from "ignorance" and represents another illusion

Seven Worldview Questions

Freddy Davis (2006) in his article, "*What is Far Eastern Thought?*" answers 7 worldview questions regarding pantheism. While not an exhaustive list, it does provide readers with a summary of the thinking which shapes this worldview.

1. What is the nature of Ultimate Reality (God)? Ultimate Reality or what many refer to as God is impersonal, pantheistic and monistic. Not only is God in everything and everything is God, everything that we see is "composed of different forms of a single substance."

2. What is the nature of material reality (the world and everything in it)? The material world is not personal, not real, and desirous of oneness.

3. What is humanity? Humans and their personalities do not really exist; both are illusions.

4. What happens to a person at death? When humans die, their life force is reabsorbed into the life force or cosmos through reincarnation.

5. Why is it possible to know anything at all? Real knowledge is not really possible; therefore, your observations are not as you imagine.

6. How do we know what is right or wrong? In the cosmos, one finds perfection. Thus, good and evil are not real.

7. What is the meaning of human history? Time does not exist. What is perceived as time is a series of cyclical events that keep repeating. (2)

In the Words of a Pantheist

Remember, a worldview simply points to a person's frame of reference. It is the lens through which an individual interprets the world, culture, surroundings, and his or her personal experiences. Today, while some practitioners would embrace the notion of a pantheistic worldview, many other practitioners would deny the connection. Some practitioners would resonate with the words of American architect, Frank Lloyd Wright, "I believe in God, only I spell it Nature" (Pantheist Association for Nature). They would be drawn into the idyllic narrative of writer and naturalist, John Borroughs who writes:

> If we do not go to church so much as did our fathers, we go to the woods much more, and are much more inclined to make a temple of them than our fathers did. We now use the word *nature* very much as our fathers used the word God, and I suppose, back of it we mean the power that is everywhere present and active, and in whose lap the visible universe is held and nourished. It is a power that we can see and touch and hear, and we realize every moment of our lives how

absolutely we are dependent on it. (Pantheist Association for Nature).

But suppose for the sake of argument, we replace the word "nature" with the word, "Reiki." Suddenly, it begins to resemble the current descriptions practitioners use to describe Reiki.

On the other hand, there are practitioners who embrace theism which maintains a belief in an infinite and transcendent God who creates and sustains all things. They would initially find agreement with the observations of Paul Harrison, author and environmentalist who writes, "When theists look at a forest, or at a cell, or at a galaxy, they feel that they are contemplating the reflected glory of an invisible creator, or they are staring at God's impenetrable veil…" (Pantheist Association for Nature). "Yes," most theists would agree. Citing the Bible, they might also reflect on Psalms 19:1 (NIV), "The heavens declare the glory of God." It would be a clear affirmation that they perceive creation as distinct from the Creator. However, it is the second part of Harrison's statement which should generate some concern. He adds, "…When pantheists do so [look at a forest, cell or galaxy], they are directly witnessing the glory of divine being. They are gazing on the unveiled face of God." In other words, the "cosmos," "nature," the "universe" is elevated from something that was created to actually being named *God!* Many practitioners of Reiki, especially those who allege Christian moorings might ignore this fact and still argue that they see God as distinct from nature, the cosmos, or the universe. Thus, to embrace Reiki, they must assent (consciously or unconsciously) to using a name (like Energy Medicine, or Energy Fields Therapy—life energies) or term [or they must subscribe to a form] that is repackaged in particular for Western audiences. What predates the legendary Christianized version of Mikao Usui's Reiki could be referred to as Reiki's older sister, Therapeutic Touch. This was a "form" that many accepted, especially those in nursing.

Therapeutic Touch: If it Quacks like a Duck... 7

Therapeutic Touch was first taught as a graduate level course at the distinguished New York University. The course was entitled, "Frontiers in Nursing: The Actualization of Potential for Therapeutic Human Field Interaction." As a prototype in this country, the course was very popular, and many other schools imported it because of the prestige of New York University. There were several reasons that Therapeutic Touch became readily accepted. As a practice, it appeared natural and non-invasive; it seemed to work; it was well-received by many in the nursing community; it closely resembled the Christian practice of laying-on of hands. Furthermore, in its presentation, it appeared to have scientific validation.

Therapeutic Touch Defined

One might ask, "Exactly, what is Therapeutic Touch?" According to one of its founders, Dolores Krieger, "Therapeutic Touch is a contemporary interpretation of several ancient healing practices. These practices consist of learned skills for consciously or sensitively modulating human energies" (Krieger 1993, 11). It allegedly brings alleviation of pain and psychosomatic maladies, facilitates the body's innate healing ability, and provides the sensation of relaxation. It is mediated through a type of indirect laying on of hands. According to nurse practitioner Kevin Courcey:

Therapeutic Touch was developed in the early 1970's by Dolores Krieger RN, a professor of nursing. Krieger and co-founder Dora Kunz stated that the human body is kept alive and vital by a force called *prana* (a Sanskrit term meaning "vital force") and that this energy flows around and through the body and is channeled by *charkas,* a system of non-physical energy centers in the body... Current practice is based on the assumption that the physical body is surrounded by an energy field that trained practitioners can detect, assess, and manipulate, and that imbalances in this energy field result in illness or pain, which Therapeutic Touch can treat. (2000, n.p.)

Therapeutic Touch Training

Step One: Centering

There are four steps in administering Therapeutic Touch. They include centering, assessment, unruffling, and modulation. In describing the first step, Dolores Krieger in Therapeutic Touch (1993) reports that what is being centered is the healer's consciousness. She explains, "Centering is an act of researching, a going on within to explore the deeper level of yourself. In this act of journeying inward, you can learn, like a yogi, to trace or follow the energy flows of your own consciousness in a quest to understand your own being and your relationship to the universe" (17). She stresses the importance of centering because "...you, as the healer, are the sole determiner of what will happen during the therapeutic process.... How the process proceeds depends upon your ability to discriminate among the subtle cues of the healee's energy-field dynamics" (17). Often to foster a relaxed and tranquil state, meditative practices like the repeating of a mantra are employed.

Step Two: Assessment

The second step is assessment in which practitioners "scan" the energy field of the healee. According to Krieger (1993), "...human beings are open energy systems: we do not stop at our skins" (22). In the assessment process, practitioners place their hands with palms down approximately two to four inches above the healee and systematically scan the entire body in search of energy blockages. Krieger references the East Indian *"chakras"* system, non-physical energy transformers, allegedly located in the human energy field. These energy centers represent various levels of consciousness. According to Sharon Fish (1995) in "Therapeutic Touch: Healing Science or Psychic Midwife, "Areas of pain and accumulated tension or inflammation are believed to be perceived in the hands as various sensations such as tingling, unusual pressure or pulsation, and heat or coldness. These sensations are thought to reflect blocked or accumulated energy" (2). The hands are able to detect the sensations because Krieger maintains that there are secondary chakras located in the palms of the hands (23).

Step Three: Unruffling

The third step is unruffling. In this step, the practitioner's hands are more animated as he or she seeks to "decongest" or break up areas that are blocked. In addition to "decongesting" an area using circular gestures, Krieger (1993) notes that unruffling facilitates "…changing an energy pattern, or cooling an elevated body temperature or area of inflammation"(179). If the accumulated energy is not redistributed to an area with less energy, the practitioner gets rid of the extra energy by vigorously shaking their hands and sweeping energy towards the feet.

Step Four: Modulation

The fourth and final step is modulation. In this step, there is a definite transfer of energy from the practitioner to the healee, or the practitioner redirects the energy of the healee. At times, the practitioner's hands will remain over areas where a blockage was initially recognized. The session, which can generally last from fifteen minutes to a half hour is complete when the practitioner intuitively senses it is over.

The Therapeutic Touch Experience

Often when Therapeutic Touch is discussed, there are many anecdotal stories of recipients having sensations of tingling, heat, and "hands all over their body." However, the practitioner also seems to benefit from the interaction. Krieger (1979) shares the experience of a practitioner who vividly described a session:

> The ambient temperature in the room is cool. I inhale deeply, feeling the coolness of the air rush in the tip of my nostrils I continue focusing on the air going through my nasal passages and into my chest. In...out.... I am breathing slowly and deeply. I gradually become aware of a large, dark abyss located in the center of my very being and swelling within me. There is nothing present now in the environment but my client and me. It is as if we are meeting and are suspended in space-time.... Without speaking, I start the Assessment at the top of his head and work downwards. I work slowly, methodically, searching for change. I proceed carefully over the client's body. He has begun to relax now....
>
> After completing the Assessment, I return my hands to the back of his neck, where I had felt heat on the initial scanning. At this time, the heat seems to me to be even more intense, and I act to dissipate this bound energy. I place my hands over the area and feel the transfer of heat, which seems to fill up my hands. I shake the heat out with several flicks of the wrist.... We seem caught up in a timelessness.
>
> As the heat gradually dissipates, I reverse the process and focus on my hands. I slip deeper within myself calling forth positive thoughts of love to direct towards my client. I am looking at my hands. Do they really belong to me? They are tools heavily suspended in midair at the ends of my arms; they almost have an existence outside myself.
>
> Now, I am reaching a new height of awareness. Seeming to soar, I laugh joyously inside of me at the delight I am experiencing. My consciousness is not aware of the healee's

separateness. He and I are one, united, composed of flowing energy.... My client is smiling broadly.... His face is flushed, and the tenseness in his brow has disappeared. His headache is gone. We share the same joy and peace and are at one with the world. KW (130)

Psychic Soil: Therapeutic Touch Roots   8

The Legacy of Dr. Krieger and her Mentors

It is interesting to note that in much of the literature written by Christians who researched Therapeutic Touch, it was described as a form of psychic or occult healing which was designed to manipulate invisible life energies that were "out of balance" in the human energy field (Reisser, Reisser, and Weldon 1988; Gumpretcht 1988; Reisser, Mabe, and Verlarde, 2001). While some might take offense to the term "psychic," or "occult," there is much in the early foundation of Therapeutic Touch in terms of Krieger's spirituality and her mentoring to lend credence to the fact that that healing promoted in Therapeutic Touch represented a worldview which was distinct from biblical theism.

Academically, Krieger's background was in neurophysiology, and she was trained as a nurse. Her interest in hands-on healing blossomed when she became involved with her mentor, Dora Kunz in the sixties. Krieger credited the technique of laying-on of hands to Kunz. According to Fish (1995) Kunz was a self-proclaimed psychic and a past president of the Theosophical Society, an organization committed to promoting ancient religions and occult ideologies (31).

The Theosophical Society

The Theosophical society, started back in 1875 in New York by Henry Steele Olcott, Helena Blavatsky and W.Q. Judge had several goals. According to James Skeen (2002) in "Theosophy: A Historical Analysis and Refutation," one goal was to integrate ancient religion and evolutionary science (10). A second goal was to articulate their opposition to orthodox Christianity. He noted how the early founders had an "...aversion to the ideas of "human depravity, predestination, vicarious atonement, and a final judgment." (11) They [the founders] also came from spiritualistic, occult backgrounds." Jack Stahlman (2000) in "A Brief History of Therapeutic Touch" observed, "...the Society has been called the "Great Homogenizer" of ideas, blending disparate "isms" as mesmerism, spiritualism, transcendentalism, Hinduism, Buddhism, and Darwinism into a somewhat cohesive form. The influence of this amalgamation continues today and is the source of the intellectual and philosophical framework into which TT was born" (24).

Dora Kunz

In describing her mentor, Krieger (1979) pointed out that Kunz was:

> ...born with a unique ability to perceive subtle energies around living beings. From the time she was a child, she studied the function and control of these energies under the tutelage of Charles W. Leadbeater, one of the great seers (occultists) of the twentieth century. Through the years, she has studied these abilities in depth so that they have become like a fine instrument in her hands which she can turn on or off at will. (4)

By her own admission, "Kunz reported that she was born fully encased in a caul, a fetal birth membrane that traditionally heralds clairvoyant and psychic abilities." She noted how both her mother and grandmother "had psychic abilities" and how she was "expected to meditate upon...complex and abstract ideas in a special room set aside for just that purpose" (Stahlman, 27). Kunz acknowledged that she developed an awareness of her "alleged psychic abilities" around the age of seven and was encouraged by her mentor, Charles Leadbeater who was a fellow "clairvoyant" and a "prolific theosophical writer" (Stahlman, 27).

When Kunz and Krieger began to collaborate in the sixties, Kunz was working with Oskar Estabany, a theosophical healer who had been a Colonel in the Hungarian cavalry. Utilizing the laying-on of hands, Estabany initially worked with healing horses. Buoyed by his success with horses, he eventually began healing humans by adding prayer to his hands-on healing. He strongly felt that his ability to heal came from him channeling the spirit of Jesus Christ (Stahlman, 31). Krieger had the opportunity to observe him directly when she worked in the capacity as a nurse, gathering case histories and monitoring the patients that came to Estabany for healing. Krieger admired his work and commented that "a felt energetic intensity was quite perceptible upon entering the house" (Krieger, 1979, 6). Encouraged by his success, Krieger began to search the literature for others who had utilized the laying-on of hands. Over time, she discovered the work of Bernard Grad, a biochemist. Grad had experimented with mice and barley seeds in which Estabany had used the laying-on of hands. She was also influenced by Sr. Justa Smith's work, "Paranormal Effects on Enzyme Activity" who had also collaborated with Estabany. Having observed the studies of Grad and Smith, Krieger (1975) admitted that she felt, "…challenged …as a practitioner, teacher, and nurse researcher" (785).

Consequently, Krieger retreated again to the literature to attempt to context what she had observed concerning the laying-on of hands. Although she surveyed literature from the West, she did not find a plausible explanation regarding healing. Thus, she ventured into studying healing modalities from the East to gain insight. While Krieger pointed out that Therapeutic Touch was not tied to any particular religion, it is interesting to note that Krieger is an avowed Buddhist (Stahlman, 30). For her, "The Eastern explanation of the process that occurs during the laying-on of hands lies in the Sanskrit concept of *prana* or "human life energies…. (Stahlman, 32). Krieger (1979) commented that the notion that "*prana* may be transferred from one individual to another may not be so readily apparent to us unless we have gotten into the practice and literature of hatha yoga, tantric yoga, or the martial arts of the orient." (4) Krieger reasoned that sickness or disease developed when an individual was deficient in *prana*. Thus, a "healer" with a surplus of *prana* and the desire or intent to provide healing could actually transfer life energy through the laying-on of hands to someone who was sick to bring about healing. Krieger felt strongly that healing was a natural ability, and anyone could be taught it. Thus, Krieger and Kunz made a decision to teach Therapeutic Touch to nurses who had no background in healing. As head of the Nursing Department at the New York University School of Nursing, Krieger had considerable influence. She had done considerable research, and she had the beginnings of a philosophical/theoretical framework. From its onset, however, Therapeutic Touch was not without critics. Although Krieger's research added a veneer of science, mentor, "[Martha] Rogers purported to offer a more "scientific" theoretical framework and an explanatory model of the energy fields encountered in the practice of TT" (Stahlman,. 33). Her influence served to crystallize Krieger's ideology.

Martha Rogers

Martha Rogers was an influential nurse theorist and former dean at New York University. She developed a conceptual model that described human beings as an evolving four-dimensional energy field. From that model came a belief that all humans possessed a human energy field that could be manipulated to improve health. In fact, humans were actually perceived as being energy fields. While Rogers maintained that there was no single experience that shaped her thinking, she acknowledged being influenced by Indian philosophy and history. Consistent with an eastern worldview she expressed a belief in the interrelatedness of all things. Even though the existence of a human energy field was never proven, Rogers' beliefs produced a generation of students who developed an appetite for the occult (Fish, 1995). Fish noted that these students studied such subjects as clairvoyance, precognition, Eastern mysticism, and out-of-body experiences. Krieger (1979) admitted that she honed her [healing] skills by studying yoga and Ayuvedic (Indian), Tibetan, and Chinese medicine. It was from her study of Eastern medicine that she came to believe that *prana* could be transferred from one individual to another through energy transmitters called the *chakras*.

Summary: Connecting the Dots

Both Ankerberg and Weldon (1991) concluded:

> Therapeutic Touch was developed as a result of one occultist, Dora Kunz, teaching a method of psychic healing to a willing student named Dolores Krieger. Krieger's additional research into Eastern mystical traditions and the occult refined the practice. Because what Krieger learned was a form of psychic healing, Therapeutic Touch should be labeled as such and not passed off as a scientific medicine and a form of true divine spiritual healing. (394)

If the observation made by Ankerberg and Weldon was true, how was it possible that Therapeutic Touch continued to be practiced, even by Christians? What Therapeutic Touch supporters have done over the last 35 years has been to validate this practice using science. There were many studies conducted to show the efficacy of Therapeutic Touch. **The major claims of the studies were that Therapeutic Touch was effective in wound healing, pain reduction, and relief of stress and anxiety.** However, nurse theorist Myra E. Levine (1995) in the *American Journal of Nursing* gave an early critique of Krieger's research. She commented:

> The pretense of the healers that they perform scientific therapies is unconscionable. In our struggle to achieve academic recognition as a profession, we simply can't afford to indulge in this kind of charlatanism. Therapeutic Touch

challenges the validity of modern nursing research, teaching and practice. If its practitioners insist on their healing roles, let them honestly call themselves faith healers and stop claiming they are nurses who heal. (1383)

For approximately thirty-five years, science offered a level of immunity for Therapeutic Touch. However, further research demonstrated that the scientific claims were flawed and suspect. In an unpublished work entitled, *Therapeutic Touch and Human Energy Field Therapies: A Realistic Evaluation*, O' Mathuna (2001) concluded the following: "Therapeutic Touch is not supported by years of controlled clinical studies. While many have been done, the results are inconsistent and often ambiguous. Certainly, some have produced interesting positive results. But many have shown Therapeutic Touch to be no more beneficial than a placebo" (98). Most damaging is the fact that supporters of Therapeutic Touch have maintained that it was essential to be able to detect the human energy field during assessment in order to provide the necessary intervention. However, an experiment conducted by a nine-year old Emily Rosa to determine if 21 practitioners could detect her "energy field" yielded questionable results. The practitioners could only detect her "energy field" 122 (44%) out of 280 trials. Pure chance would have would have yielded a score of 50%. The study, "A Close Look at Therapeutic Touch" was published in the prestigious *Journal of the American Medical Association*. (Rosa L, Rosa E, Sarner L, Barrett S, 1998) The response of the Therapeutic Touch community was that the "energy field" no longer had to be detected. What was most important was the healer's intent.

What was most disheartening about the research that now invalidated scientific claims about Therapeutic Touch was that, in a postmodern culture, much of the criticism has fallen on deaf and uncritical ears. Ankerbeg and Weldon made an astute observation in 1991 regarding Therapeutic Touch, "There is little doubt that the practice of Therapeutic Touch is laying the groundwork for the acceptance of more traditional psychic healers in our hospitals"

(396). Fish concurred by stating, "Therapeutic Touch is also playing midwife, helping bring to birth in nursing a host of spiritually illegitimate and dangerous practices that include mediumship and more. Those who say they can practice and divorce themselves from its occult associations need to be reminded that apart from the occult, TT would not exist" (10).

In less than two decades, their observation has come true. One can go to any major hospital in the United States and find health care services that have included the practice of Reiki and a variety of other alternative therapies. Moreover, in some hospitals, it has been possible to find a shaman (medicine man/woman) performing healing rites over a sick patient. Yes, Reiki has made significant impact as a safe, non-invasive healing art, and the numbers of those giving and receiving Reiki has continued to grow.

Reiki Claims Based on Research: Shield or Achilles' Tendon? 9

Reiki and Scientific Studies

Mikao Usui clearly stated "**Reiki is a spiritual method** that goes beyond medical science" (Petter, 17). Although Usui's statement was accurate and extremely telling, many practitioners have attempted to excise Reiki's spiritual moorings by presenting the energy used in Reiki as purely scientific. Hence, the next section looks at some of the literature that presents Reiki as a scientific, non-invasive, energetic healing modality.

One such study conducted by Brenlan, Levine, Rodriguez et al. (1993), in *Complementary Therapies in Medicine,* sought to measure the effect of Reiki and Le-Shan (a type of distance healing) on post-operative pain. Their studies included a group of 21 subjects with impacted lower third teeth. The subjects were assigned to either a control group or a treatment group. *The authors' findings indicated that the treatment group reported lower levels of pain intensity and higher levels of pain relief, allowing them to conclude that Reiki and Le-Shan may significantly reduce post-operative pain as it relates to the extraction of impacted third molar teeth.* It is interesting to note that the group treated with Reiki and Le-Shan was given an oral analgesic (painkillers) and a rescue analgesic if pain persisted.

Another study that was shrouded in subjectivity was done by Thornton (1996), who published a thesis on the "Effects of Energetic Healing on Female Nursing Students." She hypothesized that female-nursing students would report feeling less stress and anxiety, increased personal power, and increased well-being after having a Reiki treatment. One group received treatment from a Reiki practitioner while another group received a bogus Reiki treatment from someone who had not been trained in Reiki. The findings indicated that the three hypotheses were unsubstantiated. However, it was discovered that both groups had lowered anxiety levels based on STAI (**State-Trait Anxiety Inventory**) anxiety assessment tool. In the absence of finding any objective evidence, a post-treatment assessment was performed and participants were asked open-ended questions to respond to how the treatment made them "feel." The participants commented about feeling "warm," "relaxed," "sleepy," and having "reflective states of consciousness." According to Thornton, *"The Reiki group reported feeling sensations of tingling/electricity, sensations of floating, experiencing a state of oneness with the Reiki practitioner, undergoing a life review, and experiencing a complete emptying out of the mind" (13–15).*

An attempt at a more objective study by Wendy Wertzel (1989), in "Reiki Healing: A Physiologic Perspective," sought to test the effect of Reiki on hemoglobin (the oxygen carrying pigment in red blood cells) and hematocrit (percentage of red blood cells in a sample)levels of participants undergoing first degree Reiki training and those levels for participants not undergoing Reiki training. The conclusion was that those receiving Reiki training had changes in their levels and those without Reiki training showed no significant change in their blood levels.

Another study by Engebretson and Wardell (1997), entitled "Biological Correlates of Reiki Touch Healing" in the *Journal of Advanced Nursing*, had the goal of "testing a framework of relaxation or stress reduction as a mechanism of touch therapy" (439). The study examined physiological and biochemical effects after receiving 30 minutes of Reiki; it included 23 participants and utilized biological markers such as blood pressure, salivary IgA, cortisol (stress hormone), muscle tension, and skin temperature. Reiki sessions were given to the participants. Once again, anxiety levels were reduced, salivary levels rose, but the salivary cortisol as well as the skin temperature levels were not statistically significant. *It was concluded that the findings suggested "both biochemical and physiological changes in the direction of relaxation"* (Engebretson and Wardell, 439).

In a series of five experiments, Wirth et al. (1996), attempted to measure the potential accelerated effects of Reiki, Therapeutic Touch (TT), Le Shan, and, intercessory prayer on wound healing in humans. Reiki was given to the TT practitioners on alternate days in conjunction with biofeedback, along with an hour of guided imagery, and distant Le Shan healing. While the first two studies using Therapeutic Touch showed an accelerated rate of wound healing for the treatment group, the *study using Reiki showed no significant treatment effect. In conclusion, the overall results were inconclusive and did not establish Reiki, in particular, as an effective aid in the acceleration of healing dermal wounds.*

Other Studies

R.A. Bucholtz (1996) conducted a single-blind crossover study to examine the effects of Reiki touch in comparison to casual touch. The study included six subjects who functioned as a control group. Pre- and post-pain measurements were taken. *Results indicated that pain decreased over time with Reiki treatments. However, the results were not statistically significant.*

Reiki as Adjunctive or Complementary Therapy

Some studies on Reiki sought to integrate Reiki as a complementary therapy for life. Marlene Bullock (1997), in *The American Journal of Palliative Care*, gave a case study example of how Reiki was invaluable in hospice care for a patient with a limited life expectancy. *Reiki was attributed to helping "Tom" manage his pain and anxiety. "[Although] he is confused at times, continues to ambulate with a walker, and is on MS Contin 3000mg, ... he is living well with his cancer...with the Reiki and his intent..."* (Bullock, 33).

Reiki in Clinical Settings

Sawyer (1998), Miles and True (2003), Biali (2002), and Alandydy and Alandydy (1999) highlighted the use of Reiki in clinical settings. In particular, Alandydy and Alandydy in the *Journal of Nursing Care Quality* emphasized the use of Reiki in Portsmith Regional Hospital as an adjunct to patients after surgery. The goal was to bring about the restoration of energy and balance and to facilitate the body's innate healing mechanisms. Patients were given the option of receiving Reiki for 15 minutes after surgery. In 1998, more than 872 patients opted to have the 15-minute session to "settle and center themselves before and after surgery" (1) *The findings indicated that stress levels were reduced and less pain medication was needed after surgery.* It was unclear as to how these findings were measured. It is interesting to note that the Alandydy and Alandydy study indicated that Reiki was an ancient Buddhist practice commencing 2500 years ago. However, they added, "While not a religion, Reiki honors the spirituality of the ... Spirit connection" (1).

Nield-Anderson and Ameling (2000) reported the benefits of Reiki for patients who were in hospice care. Feelings of nausea and emotional trauma were reduced resulting from the relaxing effects promoted by Reiki. Moreover, interactions between caregivers and recipients were enhanced because of emotional stress reduction facilitated by Reiki treatments (24).

Reiki Benefits to Nurse Practitioners and Patients

Robin Gallob (2003), in the *Journal of the New York State Nurses Association*, suggested that Reiki was a practice that allowed the nurse practitioner to take care of self. Since the practitioners were not using their own energy but were "linked with a healing energy outside themselves," their Ki energy was not depleted (10). Consequently, they did not need to be replenished after a treatment. In referencing Barnett and Chambers (1996), *Gallop stressed the practitioners' feelings of tingling, warmth, and vibrations when administering Reiki treatments. Moreover, the recipient of Reiki treatment reported feeling "heat or cold, waves of energy, tingling, heavi-*

ness, or floating sensations. Profound relaxation and time distortion are common experiences, as are emotional responses such as peace or bliss (Barnett & Chambers 1996, Bullock 1997, Engebretson & Wardell 2002, Mansour et al. 1998)" (10).

When describing Reiki, an emphasis has been placed on what recipients and practitioners feel. Some have talked about feeling waves of energy, warmth, heat, and tingling sensations. What is interesting to note is that there are individuals who have experienced Christ-based healing. They have talked about feeling some similar sensations. However, in the next few chapters, distinctions will be made about the source and purpose of the healing.

Reiki as Adjunct in Psychotherapy

If the discussion of Reiki were limited to physical healing, perhaps it would not initially invoke the attention of Christian counselors who frequently deal with the emotional, psychological, and spiritual needs of counselees. However, as previously mentioned, Reiki, in its inception was presented by its founder to address "all diseases, whether they have been caused by psychological or physical factors..." and had the ability to "heal bad habits and psychological disorders" (Petter, 16). Hence, there were varieties of psychological problems that Reiki practitioners sought to address. In addition to stress and anxiety, others included depression and trauma-related disorders. On occasion, these problems were precipitated by physical problems. Keler and Wellman (1997) emphasized that Reiki was used by participants who generally had higher levels of education with professional or managerial positions. Of this group, 27% used Reiki to address emotional problems.

Barnett and Chambers (1996), in *Reiki: Energy Medicine,* addressed how Reiki was beneficial in psychotherapy. Barnett, as a Reiki Master and medical social worker, stressed how in her practice Reiki hastened the psychotherapeutic process by evoking insight and counsel concerning the counselees' problem and by facilitating the release of "emotional residue ... from the body's cells" that accompanied the problem (76). The emotional release produced "well-being and empowerment" (76). She added that many psychotherapists who wanted to incorporate modalities like Reiki into their practice became "licensed as ministers, since most states allow clergy to touch clients in the process of their healing ministry" (79). Barnett commented that based on her training and employment in social work, "the fundamental principle guiding my Reiki psychotherapy is that all healing comes from within.... The client...is powerful and whole, having all the answers within. Reiki supports the accessing of this inner wisdom" (79).

Susan Golden, a Reiki student of Barnett's and a psychologist, interviewed psychotherapists to determine the benefits of integrating Reiki into their practice. Dr. Golden summarized the three primary results. They included: (1) "a deepening of ... therapeutic work and a quicker reestablishment of emotional equilibrium ..." for the client in addition to the ability for clients to persevere and resolve painful issues, (2) clients were more aware of images that served as metaphors to problematic areas; understanding the imagery allowed the client to change the outcomes, and (3) clients were able to discern the connection of emotional or psychological problems to physical symptoms (Barnett and Chambers, 83). *It was concluded that Reiki improved the efficacy of psychotherapy, energized rather than depleted therapists thereby reducing their levels of stress, heightened intuitive abilities, and helped the development of "more detached compassion"* (84). It is noteworthy that Birnbaum (1979) observed that in Buddhist healing a "fundamental attitude of Buddhism [was] dispassionate compassion" (Birnbaum, 17).

Reiki and Depression

Shore (2001) conducted a study that traced the long-term effects of Reiki, also cited as energetic healing, on depression and self–perceived stress. Emphasis was placed on the fact that current research verified "conventional treatment of clinical depression remains less than optimal" (43). She referenced Leskowitz's recognition of a flawed medical model that failed to "account for the inner life of human beings, in both the psychological and spiritual realms" (43). Moreover, she offered that proponents of energetic modalities like Reiki felt the physical and mental health was improved using Reiki, which also supported "personal growth through a deeper connection to the spiritual aspects of life... " (43). She argued strongly that health was positively influenced by spiritual and religious experiences and lamented, "Despite numerous attempts to understand the phenomenon of energetic healing as a form of spiritual healing and despite the number of significant findings in energetic healing research, it remains overlooked as a viable therapy by the mainstream medical community" (43). An apparent contradiction was that while owning the spiritual nature of Reiki, Shore still sought to measure its effects empirically. Although Shore talks about spirituality, she does not define it. Webster (2002) defines "spiritual" as "(1) relating to sacred matters, (2) concerned with religious values, (3) relating to supernatural beings or phenomena." In a pluralistic culture, spirituality is framed by one's worldview. The spirituality that Shore references is one in which the worldview is pantheistic; the experiences are mystical; the method of gaining spiritual information is occult (hidden).

For the purpose of analysis, Shore used a 3 x 3 factorial MANOVA in addition to the Beck Depression Inventory, Beck Hopelessness, and Perceived Stress scales. There were 46 participants who were assigned to one of three groups. The groups included hands-on-Reiki, distance Reiki, and placebo distance Reiki. The participants were seen for 60 or 90 minutes over a period of six weeks. Prior to receiving Reiki, the initial testing did not demonstrate any distinctions among the groups. After receiving Reiki, findings indicated that the treatment group displayed decreased symptoms of psychological distress, and the distinctions seemed continuous a year later. It appeared that those who received Reiki at a distance had the greatest reduction in symptoms. The conclusion drawn was that Reiki, as a form of energetic healing, could be effective as an adjunct in long-term reduction of depression, hopelessness, and stress as evidenced by scales used. The challenge with this study is that there is no way of tracking what precipitated the patients' depression and the factors that influenced symptom reduction.

Reiki and HIV/AIDS Treatment

Robert Schmehr (2003) emphasized the clinical application of using Reiki to enhance treatment for individuals suffering with HIV. Schmehr, a psychotherapist and Reiki II practitioner, served as a director of Complementary Therapy at an HIV Center in New York. He generated a case study report about a 62-year-old man. He was diagnosed with AIDS and was initially seeking medical attention. Other problems diagnosed by a psychiatrist were depression, anxiety, and substance abuse. His cocaine usage accelerated to 2 grams daily after his partner of seventeen years died from AIDS (120).

Aided by a social worker, he participated in an out-treatment drug program and commenced psychotherapy. Refusing to take psychotropic medication and expressing an interest in "natural healing, meditation, and spirituality," he was referred by his psychotherapist to a hospital that did Reiki trainings (120). He was initiated into level one Reiki and received Reiki treatments twice a week. An hour of Reiki was given by clinic volunteers, and he treated himself for an hour. He relayed to both his physician and psychotherapist that "Reiki self-treatments [were] extremely relaxing and enjoyable, and that it helped him to maintain his sobriety and work through his depression" (120). Approximately two years after initiation into Reiki, he stopped psychotherapy and reported a continued cessation of drug use. He was then employed part-time and voluntarily provided Reiki to individuals with AIDS. Schmehr was clear that there was no direct correlation between the medical improvements and the benefits of Reiki in the treatment of AIDS. *However, the conclusion drawn by the physician, psychotherapist, and patient was that Reiki self-treatment "was the single greatest factor contributing to his successful behavior change" (118). Although the man still had AIDS, it was suggested, "the patient is thriving according to quality of life and productivity assessments" (118).*

Reiki's Scientific Validation

In most of the reports or studies concerning Reiki, Reiki has had no effect, a modest effect, or questionable effects, which need more scientific validation. Although some practitioners value the support of science, some literature has suggested that there are Reiki practitioners, as well as recipients, who are not necessarily interested in scientific validation. Engebretson and Wardell (2002) commented, "Despite the lack of theoretical understanding and the equivocal [unclear] nature of the research, use of touch therapies has continued to increase." Kelner, Boon, Wellman, and Welsh (2002) examined the views of three different groups who practiced complementary and alternative medicine. One group was Reiki practitioners. When asked about effectiveness, "the necessity to show that their therapies actually had a positive effect on the health outcomes of patients…" there were a range of views (236). However, the Reiki group appeared least interested in evaluating effectiveness. The researchers noted:

> They [Reiki practitioners] found the notion puzzling and troublesome and were uncertain how to reply to our questions about it. With one exception, they considered it unimportant to prove that Reiki works and were also convinced that conventional outcome measures would be inappropriate for their form of healing. They explained that Reiki Therapy is a form of spiritual growth based on energy and that scientific research on effectiveness is too mechanistic to fit their paradigm. As one respondent commented, "Reiki speaks for itself." (236–237)

Pat Kennedy (2001), working as a nurse and therapist, reported the benefits of using Reiki with torture victims in *Complementary Therapies in Nursing and Midwifery*. She was pleased that some doctors in Europe "are willing to accept therapies which have limited evidence to substantiate results" (7). However, she offered, "But surely there must come a time when the results speak for themselves (7).

Miles, in "Reiki Vibrational Healing," added a paradoxical twist to the discussion on Reiki research. As the founder and director of the Institute for the Advancement of Complementary Therapies and a researcher, she seemed to support Reiki research relentlessly. However, in disclosing the recent research findings of Richardson Davidson, who linked the practice of meditation to "increased prefrontal lobe brain stimulation ... and enhanced immunity" (Miles 2003, 81), she made an ironic comment. While acknowledging the superlative nature of the research, she suggested:

> It's time to look across modalities. Do we have to do all the research on Therapeutic Touch and then all the same research on Reiki?... Or can we look at the commonalities of these practices?... Limited research resources could be put to better use if we learned more about the healing process... and to what extent can we generalize research findings. (82)

It was an odd request coming from a person who believed that Reiki was "the only modality in which access to primordial consciousness is institutionalized" (82). Given Reiki's alleged distinctiveness and current inconclusive scientific validation, it would seem wise to continue researching it instead of accepting the findings of similar energy modalities in which studies were still shrouded with questionable scientific results. It would be fodder for medical malpractice if the same attitude were taken about prescription drugs that yielded questionable results.

Current Research

It has been eight years since Miles advocated that research findings from "past" studies be "generalized" in favor of Reiki. However, many supporters have continued to push for scientific validation with results that have not significantly advanced Reiki's standing in the scientific community. So, Jiang, and Qin (2008) concluded after conducting 24 studies that included Reiki, Healing Touch, and Therapeutic Touch, that "touch therapies may have a modest effect in pain relief." However, more studies are needed. Assefi, Bogart, Goldberg, and Buchwald (2009) received a government grant to study the effects of Reiki for the treatment of fibromyalgia and concluded that Reiki as well as touch had no effect on pain nor did it improve the symptoms of fibromyalgia. Again, it was recommended that more "rigorous" studies be done on Reiki before recommending it as a treatment for patients with chronic pain. Ernst, Lee, and Pittler, (2008) did a systematic review of randomized clinical trials to evaluate the effectiveness of Reiki on any medical condition. Of the 205 relevant articles, only 9 met the review criteria. It was concluded that "...evidence is insufficient to suggest that Reiki is an effective treatment for any condition. Therefore, the value of Reiki remains unproven" (953). Of course, there continue to be studies that support limited effectiveness of Reiki. But as demonstrated in previous studies, the usual suggestion is always to conduct more research.

The reality is that Reiki, under the auspices of pseudo-science, has continued the process of becoming institutionalized in settings where people are already very vulnerable. Its institutionalization was confirmed by Gallob (2003, 9) who offered, "[Reiki] has ... found its way to healthcare professionals and into medical institutions (Alandydy & Alandydy 1999, Barnett & Chambers 1976, Mills 2001, Rand, 1997)." With the possibility of pain, anxiety, and stress reduction, patients/clients are willing to try almost anything if they have been convinced that they might feel better. Beyond being made to feel better, perhaps the most effective means of spreading Reiki has been the almost unanimous presentation in the literature that vehemently supports the claim that "Reiki does no harm." Even when Reiki is dismissed as "nonsense," the connotation has been that it is no more effective than a placebo, suggesting of course that placebos are harmless. However, a closer examination of those who have had more direct experiences with Reiki clearly indicate that Reiki can and does cause harm. While it may not manifest immediately, there is Reiki "fruit" that grows over time.

Part Two

You Shall Know The Truth…
Concerning Biblical Healing

Introduction to Biblical Healing 10

Pastor Norris

Pastor Norris had many experiences with various forms of spiritual, emotional, and physical healing. He was miraculously healed of the potentially fatal Lou Gehrig's disease when in response to hearing the voice of God telling him to worship and praise him early one morning, he obeyed. Again, this was not mediated through the laying-on of hands but was in response to submitting to the counsel of the Lord. However, he shared a dramatic physical healing that took place for his wife from prayer, anointing with oil, and the laying-on of hands. He began to recount the details of God's intervention in his wife's life by questioning me:

> You've seen my wife, you saw her today? [I nodded] I don't know if you noticed, but she walks with a limp. The story behind that is twenty-two years ago she was involved in an auto accident, smashed into a tree and broke her neck. Uh, she was—we were told—I was told that she was not going to live throughout the day. They showed me that CAT scans and the x-rays that showed that the bones in C-5 and C-6 fractured in such a way that they cut across the spinal cord and severed—basically severed the head from the rest of the body. Spinal cord tissue does not regenerate. If you cut your hand, it heals, it regenerates. If you break a bone, it regenerates. Spinal

cord tissue doesn't regenerate. If it's dead, it's dead. To this day if we take an x-ray of [my wife's] neck, there's no connection between her head and the rest of the body. And I joke with her about that a lot. (Laugh) But the point is when she had that accident, they told her she was going to die. She knew she wasn't because she'd heard the Lord tell her as she was moving toward the tree, 'This is not unto death.' And the Lord told me that she would walk again, even though we had her transferred to Russ Institute in New York.... [It's the] finest spinal cord injury center in the world. We moved her there, and they told us the same thing everybody else did—. Well, not only do we not know why she's alive, but there's no possibility that she will ever use anything below the neck again....

She was going to be—she is quadriplegic. She is a quadriplegic—a walking, moving quadriplegic but for that moment in time, for December 14, '82 until May of '83 nothing below the neck moved. There was no fingers, no toes, no arms, legs nothing moved. Uh, bladder was strictly by catheterization and bowel was by digital bowel management. And that was the only way that anything worked. Even breathing—we still don't understand how she breathed because nothing below here was supposed to function at all. But it did. But there was no chance she would ever walk. But when I told pastors—when I told the doctors there that I had [heard] a voice from the Lord that she was going to walk again, they called in psychiatric help for us because they knew that I was nuts and my wife was nuts too. [According to the doctors] We were involved in the denial pattern, uh, there was—there was just no chance. But we brought a group of people from the church about 30 or 40 people from our church in New Jersey—stormed into the hospital one night, poured oil all over Sarah, laid hands, this was a Wednesday night—Thursday morning the fingers and toes are back, within a week, everything was kind of functioning well and about three weeks later she walked out of the hospital.

[I commented that this healing defied medical science.]

> Yeah, physiologically, anatomically, there is no logical reason why she should walk, or even why she should be alive....
> The result of it...mention the result, that's why I told the story—those—the doctors, especially two of them, I can't remember the name of the second in command, but the top dog at the hospital was named Lars Ragnarson from Iceland. And he was one of our chief mockers, you know? "There's no way that she's ever going to walk" until the day Sarah walked. And then that was the day he became a Christian.... Everybody on that floor got saved! ... Oh.—it was impossible not to be saved. Yeah! What are you going to do? You've been working with this lady for six months and she's totally a quadriplegic and suddenly the next day she's standing up talking to you and she's walking! ... Oh, as a result of that there were scores of people in that hospital who gave their hearts to the Lord! ... Ragnarson came in to see Sarah the next day and she happened to have the Bible laying on the table next to the bed and he looked at her and he said, "I guess that works."

In telling the story, Pastor Norris emphasized the fact that when Christ-based healing occurs, it is supposed to have an evangelizing and transformative effect that draws individuals towards Jesus.

Pastor Alexis' (physical healing)

Pastor Alexis recalled a family history of cancer and the fear that accompanied it. She thought at some point that she too would develop cancer. She remembered:

> So I go to this service one night at this church and in the middle of the sermon, the man for no reason at all, it didn't go with his text, talks about how the devil tries to put a fear of cancer on people and that, though his parents died of cancer, he made the decision he would never die of cancer and he said,

'nor will I be tormented from the spirit of fear of cancer,' and immediately I knew I had that problem. I wasn't demon possessed; God was in my life; the Holy Spirit was in my heart, but I knew that I was really oppressed on a daily basis with this fear of cancer. So as soon as he got done preaching, I ran up, "Pray for me, pray for me," so he prayed for me and took authority over the spirit of cancer, fear of cancer, and I was set free. So a few weeks later I'm in the shower and I find a lump in my left breast and I'm like "Devil, you're a liar, I just got set free from the fear of cancer, what more could you bring to me than the fear of breast cancer." So I knew in my testimony it was a spiritual battle. And when I teach this and preach this, I tell women not to follow my example, not to walk in my steps, but to get a word from God for themselves because if you try to do what I did without hearing from God, you'll die.... The devil will kill you, and you will be dead.

So I prayed and I said, "Lord I know this is a spiritual attack; it's nothing more than the enemy trying to come back and take the victory you gave me over the spirit of fear; I'm going to talk to my husband and, if he's in agreement, I'm not going to go to a doctor. I'm going to stand in faith; I'm going to believe God. I'm going to have prayer, and I'm going to stand on the Word that 'by your stripes I am healed.'" So, I go to my husband: I share it with him. He says, "I agree with you; let's touch and agree," so the two of us prayed, in agreement, and we decided not to tell anyone that I was fighting this particular fight. I have some real good reasons for that, but we decided not to tell anyone we were fighting this fight of faith but to just keep it between the two of us and to pray and we did go to our pastor.... Well, I had no idea the battle I was going to have to fight. This little lump began to grow and became an actual mass in my breast and I was in pain 24/7, couldn't sleep on my stomach, had trouble wearing certain garments, really painful. And I kept praying and saying, "God, I'm healed," and I kept quoting all the Scriptures and doing what I call

Christian aerobics, you know, and I prayed the prayer of faith and I rebuked the devil and I worshipped and I did all the gymnastics and I got no better. I got worse.

Finally, after a long time, my husband went and told my daughter and my daughter came to me and broke down crying and said, "Mom, I want you to be at my wedding. I want you to be a grandmother to my children. If you die now with cancer, then I'm not going to have you." My daughter went off on me. So she said, "Mom, please get a mammogram," so I said, 'I'll do it.' So I went and I knew before I got there what was going to be the results. They'd take the mammogram; they'd come out, the films not even dry, the doctor says, "You have a large mass in your left breast and we want to call in a breast specialist; we want to do a biopsy...." So, I said, 'I'll tell you what, it's been here this long, set it for tomorrow. Give me one more day.' So I go home and I'm really upset, and the next day I had a board meeting at my house with some of the women in the ministry. And I decided after all this time standing in faith—alone...to tell them I need help. So I broke down; I'm sobbing. I said, 'I've got a mass in my breast, and they want to do a biopsy today and I know that it's going to go from bad to worse and they're going to end up taking off my breast and I don't want to lose it.'

So this woman lays hands on me; she's praying over me. These women, she's laying her hands on me and she says, I think it's Proverbs 26:2, I never heard this verse, "The curse causeless doesn't come," and she said, "Lord, show Alexis why the curse has come, what the causes [are] of why she's not been able to manifest healing." Just like that, God speaks to me. Now I've been so busy quoting his word instead of spending time with him; I've been so busy doing the things I was taught that I never stopped to ask him what was the problem, why wasn't I healed in the flesh because I believed in the spirit I already was, follow me? [I nodded] She prays this simple Proverbs 26:2 and God says to me, "The reason you're not healed is [that] you're in sin." I'm like, sin? I'm in sin? I'm like, what did I do?.... So I started to cry, and I said, "God, what's my sin?" Now listen to this, he says, "You're not in faith; you're in worry." He said, "All these things you're doing and saying, it's out of a worry spirit because if you really believed you were healed, you'd enter into the rest of God." He said, "Worry is a sin." Now listen to this, I repented of worry and the mass dissolved, period. I went and got a clean mammogram. The mass was gone. Now the doctors try to say you had a large cyst, and it broke. How convenient, you know what I mean? It just breaks in prayer, with no discharge or anything like that. But, here's an instance where I got a manifested healing after doing all the Christian things to do by faith, prayed the prayer of faith, rebuked the devil, but I never stopped long enough to ask God what hindered my health. Why wasn't my healing manifested? I was in the sin of worry.

Pastor Alexis (spiritual healing)

I didn't know the terms and the Christian lingo so I'm sitting here telling this evangelist, "Something happened to me, something just happened to me!" and I'm saying, "You don't understand, I'm changed, you don't get it!" I'm like, "All my sins are gone, my past is gone, and every rotten thing I ever did is gone!" I'm like—"I'm saved!" So I became this instant evangelist. You know what I mean? I'm going to get everyone saved, everybody's going to—I'm going to pull everybody out of hell. "I don't care if I burn my sleeve, you're coming with me."

Mabel (spiritual healing)

When I hear the word 'healing'…I think when Jesus came and redeemed us from sin. He also paid the price for our healing. It was part of the suffering, the crucifixion… As Scripture says, 'He was wounded for our transgression, He was bruised *for our iniquities, the chastisement of our peace was upon Him and by his stripes, we were healed. [He brings] correction for the spirit....Well, I asked Jesus to come into my heart and then I said, 'Save me,' and I had a supernatural experience where I prayed and cried out to Him and I felt renewal... I felt, uh, that I was—I felt really like I had been born again....*

Samuel (spiritual and physical healing)

He reflected on his immobilization in a hospital room; he had been told that he would never walk again. This was a point of crisis. He remembered reaching out for a tract his wife had given him. It read, "Even while laying here Jesus can visit you. All you have to do is ask...." He reflected:

> *That's what I did.... I meant it and that's just the pain and the loneliness I was in, and you know I felt—I felt within that minute I felt different, you know, I knew something had happened.... [Salvation] was my final step in accepting what God is.... You are looking at someone who was broken, shattered, who had no hope. Before I accepted him, I had no hope. Now you are looking at a person that he had put back together and he is continuing to mold and shape every day.... My [physical] healing was a bonus. It had nothing to do with me being saved, nothing to do with my relationship with him—because if he hadn't done it, I'd still—knowing what I know today right now, I would still serve him.*

Healing Defined

In continuing our discussion, it is now necessary to give a broader definition of healing which will include an expanded definition of Reiki healing in contrast to biblical healing. Webster's defined healing as: "1) the ability to make sound or whole; 2) to restore to health; 3) to cause (an undesirable condition) to be overcome; 4) to restore to original purity or integrity; 5) to return to a sound state." Those who practiced Reiki defined healing as the restoration of balance to the mind, body, and spirit. In this template of healing, much of the healing work centered on being a conduit or channel for the flow of mystical energy that was manipulated by the Reiki practitioner. Concerning this mystical energy, Reisser, Mabe and Velarde (2001) asserted:

> Historians have given the name vitalism to the notion that an invisible, nonmaterial "life force" or "life energy" flows through all things, or at least all living things. This energy is unmeasurable and undetected (by scientific methodology), it functions in a realm beyond the laws of chemistry and physics, and yet it is claimed to be the basis of all existence. In both religious and healing traditions, it goes by various names (80).

Authors John Ankerberg and John Weldon (1991) note that "this energy is invariably associated with pagan religion and occultic practitioners and has up to sixty different designations depending on the time and culture (46). Reisser, Mabe, and Verlarde concluded:

> Contemporary proponents of life energy…contend that regardless of its name, it pervades everything in the universe, unites each individual to the cosmos and is the doorway to untapped human potential. It is the root of all healing, all psychic abilities, all so-called miraculous occurrences. It is the link between science and religion. It is, in fact, what religions have called God, and is awaiting our command (80).

In contrast, however, in the Bible, there are several words utilized to define the word "healing" or "heal." Some major Old Testament Hebrew words used to suggest healing are *kehah* and *rapha,* which indicate a cure, *marpe* which suggests deliverance, and *alah* which means to bandage or plaster. In the New Testament, especially as it related to the Gospels and the ministry of Jesus, four Greek words are used to mean "heal." They include *therapeuo*, to take care of the sick and to heal miraculously; *diasozo*, to cure, preserve, or rescue; and *iaomai*, to restore to bodily health or heal spiritually (Strong 1996, s.v. "Heal").

Perhaps the most comprehensive and widely used word to indicate healing in the Gospels is the Greek word *sozo*. In the *The Hebrew-Greek Key Study Bible* (Zodhiates 1996), *sozo* means to deliver, to make whole, or to preserve from danger, loss, or destruction. Further commentary in this Bible indicated, "In the Gospels, of the instances where *sozo* is used, fourteen relate to deliverance from disease or demon possession; in twenty instances the inference is to the rescue of physical life from some impending peril or instant death; the remaining references pertain to spiritual salvation" (1676). Therefore, in the context of this research, Christ-based healing was defined in the context of illness or disease as it related to the totality of humankind—body, soul, and spirit.

In the Bible, illness and disease are used interchangeably and carry the notion of physical, mental, and spiritual/moral dysfunction as indicated by definitions found in the *Hebrew-Greek Key Study Bible*. Support is found in the meanings of New Testament Greek words *kakos, nosos, malakia, and arrostos*. Each word correlated to physical sickness, weakness, illness, or disease. However, according to Zodhiates (1595), the word *astheneia* (Mt 8:17; Heb 7:28) not only referenced weaknesses or sicknesses of the body, but it also highlights spiritual or moral weaknesses as it related to infirmities of the soul (Rom 6:19, 8:26; Heb 5:2 and 7:28). Thus, a biblical definition of healing which covered both the physical and emotional aspects of individuals was taken from the Greek word *therapeuo* which meant "to take care of the sick with relieving and curing" (Mt 12:10; Mk 1:34; Lk 6:7). It also meant "to relieve or cure disease, pain, or sorrow" *nosos* or physical sickness *malakia* miraculously. In Matthew 4:23-24, the word used for healing is *therapeuo*, and Jesus was specifically healing both disease, *nosos* and sickness, *malakia* thereby connecting these two words to the general meaning of *therapeuo*—curing the sick.

Therefore, (1) physical/mental healing is the taking care of the sick with relieving and curing of disease, pain, or sorrow miraculously. (Miraculously refers to the immediacy of the manifestation and the serving as a "sign" as reflected in the New Testament. While physical healing still serves as a sign today, healings are not always manifested immediately.) Spiritual healing of the soul, *sozo*, "specifically [reflected] salvation from eternal death, sin, and the punishment and misery consequent to sin" (Zodhiates, 1676). (Mt 1:21; Rom 5:9; Acts 4:12). Hence, (2) spiritual healing was immediate rescue, preservation, and salvation from eternal death, sin, and punishment provided through one's acceptance of Christ as Savior. Note, there are no references to balancing energy or following the path of Reiki.

In Reiki-based healing, physical or emotional healing represented an alleviation of symptoms or what many would call "cure." In some cases, even death was perceived as healing. According to practitioners, Reiki healing took place at several levels. Thus, there was discussion about healing of the mind and spirit that occurred when the mind or consciousness of the recipient became one or merged with the source of Reiki energy. This definition became clearer and other meanings emerged as the research advanced and discussions took place with practitioners. Was it still possible for a healing art to emerge that resembled the healing ministry of Jesus yet denied his power and rejected his lordship? Many adherents and practitioners believed that Reiki did just that.

The Christ-based Healing Experience 11

Invitation

If one were to attend a Christ-centered church, one that espoused belief in the Trinity, (Father, Son, Holy Spirit), the infallibility of the Bible, salvation through faith in Jesus, and the reality of the birth, death, and resurrection of Christ, one would be exposed to a variety of actors. The primary actor would be the pastor of the church who is usually responsible for "preaching" or "teaching" from the Bible. The next set of actors may include those who make up church leadership like deacons, associate ministers, elders, etc. Finally a third set of actors would be the members and visitors.

In this setting, there would normally be an "order of the service" starting perhaps with prayer, followed by group singing, sometimes referred to as "praise and worship." The goal of the prayer, singing, and praise would be to remove distractions by causing those attending to focus their attention on God—a setting of the atmosphere. Some may clap and sing while others stand and raise their hands in praise to God. Congregants may just sit or stand quietly with eyes closed in reverential piety. Others still may vocalize words of adoration or thankfulness to God. Once the atmosphere is set, the pastor or minister emerges to share the Word of God. This sharing of God's Word is perceived as God speaking through the pastor to encourage, exhort, correct, or guide those listening.

As the pastor is speaking, Christians believe that God's Spirit is moving throughout the congregation animating the words spoken by the pastor. Thus, someone may yell, "Amen." Others may nod in agreement as some sit quietly taking notes. Reactions vary based on the denomination and church culture. This description is in keeping with an evangelical church service. It is one of many approaches.

At the end of this preaching or teaching, an invitation is given. Generally, the purpose of the invitation is to offer the listener the opportunity to become a follower of Christ. At times, a pastor may ask a series of questions or make statements.

"Is God talking to you?"

"Is it time to turn your life around?"

"Man, woman, boy, or girl, today, you are not here by accident. This is a divine appointment. God loves you and wants to change your life."

In so doing, often individuals who are indecisive will respond by raising their hands. In order to then pray for them, the pastor will ask them to come to the altar, which is at the front of the church. If the pastor senses that someone is wary of coming to front of the church with others watching, that individual may be given the opportunity to meet with one of the leaders privately after the service.

Once at the altar, the pastor recites what has been called, "The Sinner's Prayer." Those at the altar repeat what the pastor says. Generally, there is recognition of having a broken relationship with God through the sin of Adam, a request for forgiveness of all sins, an acknowledgement of Jesus as God and Savior, and a commitment to follow and serve God by the power of the Holy Spirit. In this moment, the individuals who have repeated this prayer and believed it in their hearts have experienced a "spiritual healing." Their spirits which were dead to God because of the original Fall of

Adam have been healed and made alive. Thus, there is the expression, "saved" or "born again." It is in this simple but profound act of faith that a new life designed to reflect Christ begins, and God's Spirit (alive on the inside) is able to manifest.

Following this experience, for many, there are profound changes. Internal changes may include feelings of joy and admiration for God, a hunger and thirst for God's Word, and a desire to please God at any cost. External changes may include regular attendance at a place of worship to grow spiritually and avoidance of places and habits that would encourage compromise. The goal of every new believer is to grow in the knowledge of God through learning his Word as dictated in the Bible.

A Christ-based Healing Session

Several examples have already been given of spiritual healing which demonstrates salvation and physical healing. Later, more will be said concerning the work of the Holy Spirit in healing. It must be understood that in Christ-based healing, the source of the healing is God. Whether it is in hands-on-healing or prayer, the person directing the activity is simply a conduit or vessel being used by God. It is always God working behind the scene through the power of his Spirit. In Christ-based healing, the power to be a conduit of healing is a direct result of Jesus' sacrifice on the cross and the believer's relationship with God through accepting Jesus.

One of the many benefits of this relationship is receiving "gifts" of the Spirit. These gifts talked about in 1 Corinthians 12:8-13 include healing, prophecy, working of miracles in addition to others. There is disagreement in theological circles regarding if these gifts are for today. Many Christians hold to the belief that gifts ceased with the Apostles. However, others believe that the gifts are for today and have been both conduits and recipients of the workings of the Holy Spirit. It is also important to recognize that because the Holy Spirit directs all activities, Christ-centered healing cannot be performed on demand. Prayers can be recited and the laying-on-of hands can take place, but it is God who determines "when" that healing will manifest. It may be immediate; it may take place over time. It really is up to God, not the conduit who is being used as a vessel by God.

Now that it has been established that it is God that does the healing, it is equally important to clarify what "God" is being referenced. Thus, the next chapter will discuss the practice of the laying-on of hands as talked about in the Bible and the source of Christ-based healing. In order to accomplish this task, it is necessary to briefly access some of the literature to gain a better understanding of the origin of the practice.

Biblical Healing Roots: Observing the Source and Why Jesus Healed 12

The Old Testament

In talking about biblical hands-on healing, I am indebted to John F. Tipei, who has in the *Journal of the European Pentecostal Theological Association* comprehensively outlined the praxis of laying-on of hands in both the Old and New Testaments. (Given their utility for organization, the (*) topics used in this section were taken directly from his article.) Initially, he identified seven types of the laying-on of hands in the Old Testament. They included:

> (1) blessing (Gn 48:14,17; Gn 48:18); (2) healing (2 Kgs 5:11); (3) sacrifices: peace offerings (Lv 3:2; 8,13); sin offerings (Lv 4:4,15,24,29,33; 8:14; Ex 29:10; Nm 8:12; 2 Chr 29:23); burnt offerings (Lv 1:4,10; 8:18,22; Ex 29:15; Nm 8:12); and the ram of consecration (Lv 8:22; Ex 29:19); (4) The Day of Atonement ritual (Lv16:21); (5) Consecration (Nm 8:10); (6) Commissioning (Nm 27:18,23; Dt 34:9); (7) The passing of sentence upon a blasphemer (Lv 24:14; Dn 13:34). (2000, 94)

In most of the above-mentioned scriptures, the gesture of the laying-on of hands signified the theme of *identification*. The beneficiary of the laying-on of hands was being identified as the person that received blessing, judgment, or power. In the instances of the sacrifices, indirectly, the owner of the animal was identified as the beneficiary of the sacrament. More specifically, in sacrifices, the laying-on of hands demonstrated possession and ownership.

In 2 Kings 5:11, there is an indirect reference to identification and healing. The sick man Naaman identified a diseased part of his body and wanted the prophet Elisha to call on the name of God and wave his hand over the "spot" to affect a cure. His desire indicated that he felt that God could heal through Elisha's hands. However, the healing did not take place in that manner. While Naaman was healed, there was an early indication that God in his sovereignty *was not locked into any particular method* to bring about the miraculous, and an emphasis was placed on Naaman's obedience.

Sansom, (1983, 324) like Tipei, highlighted specific instances of the laying-on of hands in the Old Testament. He cited five of the seven that were indicated by Tipei. He did not include laying-on of hands for blessing or healing. However, he does make a distinction in verb usage. Apparently in the Hebrew, the verbs *sim, sit,* and *samak* were all used to indicate the laying-on of hands. He noted that the Hebrew verb *samak,* which suggested "leaning" or exercising pressure in the hands, was used in the five references while other Hebrew verbs such as *sim* and *sit* which indicated light touch, were used in blessing. A major distinction between Sansom and Tipei is seen in their thematic approach to the laying-on of hands in the Old Testament. Although Tipei saw most instances of the occurrence representing the theme of identification, Sansom argued for the dual themes: identification and transference. The theme of transference was strongly portrayed in the appointment/commissioning of Joshua to succeed Moses in Numbers 27:12-23 and Deuteronomy 34:9.

In Numbers 27: 18-23, Moses was told by God to lay hands upon Joshua and give him some of his authority. Sansom suggested that authority in this context indicated vitality and presence. He pointed out, "Some, but not all of Moses' authority is given to Joshua. . . . He is appointed to lead the people. We may therefore take the laying-on of hands as the official investiture to that task, and we may confidently accept that the hand-laying is connected with the idea of transference…" (325).

Mattingly (2001) in *Andrews University Seminary Studies* confirmed that it is generally accepted by scholars that the laying-on or the imposition of the hands had Old Testament roots. In his exegesis of both Numbers 27:12-13 and Deuteronomy 34:7, he asserted:

> It was no common individual who received laying-on of hands. [Yahweh,] the God of the spirits, of all flesh confirmed that this one to receive the laying-on of hands was a man [in] whom there was spirit. Not only was Joshua a man with an indomitable and courageous spirit, but [Yahweh] had given him a special gift of the Spirit that changed him and endowed him for leadership. Hand-laying is thus associated with a spirited man as well as with a man filled with the Spirit of [Yahweh]. (204)

It was obvious that in Joshua's commission was the notion of a divine transfer. This transfer of power was more than a symbolic gesture on the part of Moses. Mattingly alluded to the fact the laying-on of hands provided three types of transfer. He observed:

> …Joshua received a portion of Moses' honor, an extra measure of God's Spirit in the form of the spirit of wisdom and the obedience as well as the loyalty of the Israelite congregation. Laying-on of hands was the primary element which summarized and gave meaning to all other actions…. The laying-on of hands was a legal action which gave visible representation to [Yahweh's] word. While Moses laid his own hands on Joshua, [Yahweh] did the transferring. (101)

It is important to recognize that Joshua was filled with God's supernatural wisdom. Through the hands of Moses, he received a Spirit of wisdom that was outside of himself. Deuteronomy 34:9 clearly indicates that this supernatural wisdom resulted in Israel's submission to his authority and obedience to God. Thus, from the experience of Joshua, it was understood that through touch, laying-on of hands was used in the Old Testament as a way of *transferring and imparting God's divine power.*

Sullivan (1994), in *Spirit and Renewal,* noted that the laying-on of hands in the Old Testament symbolized God's blessing invoked by prayer; he alluded to Genesis 48:14-16 and Numbers 27:18, 20. He also asserted that it was a sign of communication between the one touching and the one being touched. In similar fashion, Kraiss (1983) acknowledged references to the laying-on of hands found in the Pentateuch to impart blessing and to transfer guilt or sin. In his reflection on the Old Testament, he commented, "The Old Testament passages...imply that the person who lays his hands on another is at least symbolizing the transfer of some quality of power from himself to the person from whom he is praying" (284). *It is concluded that in the examples given, the laying-on of hands in the Old Testament had spiritual significance and was ultimately designed to reflect God's purposes in some fashion.*

*Qumran Literature

Flusser (1957), in *Israel Exploration,* showed how in a Genesis Apocryphon, one of the Dead Sea Scrolls emphasized healing through the laying-on of hands. Flusser noted that to date there had been *no* record of laying-on of hands for healing found in the Old Testament, yet he acknowledged that healing through the laying-on of hands was used by the Jews during the first century B.C. or the first half of the first century, A.D. Hence, this would be before or during the time of the ministry of Jesus. Flusser also cited healing by the laying-on of hands by the Essenes, a monastic fraternity of Jews, as recorded by the historian Josephus.

*Rabbinic Literature

Although there was no specific reference to the laying-on of hands in Rabbinic literature, Tipei asserted that evidence seemed to suggest that laying-on of hands was practiced privately by the Pharisees when their students were allowed to teach publicly. This practice of the laying-on of hands served as a type of ordination.

The importance of this gesture was found in Tipei's interpretive quotation of two biblical scholars. He commented:

> According to Daube, the object of Jewish ordination is "the pouring of the ordaining scholar's personality into the scholar being ordained." For other scholars, the meaning of the laying-on of hands in Jewish ordination is the transference of Moses' spirit (or Divine Spirit) down through generations in unbroken sequence. (99)

Tipei submitted that while the interpretations could not be supported by Rabbinic literature, "there are at least two midrashim which provide positive evidence that the laying of hands in the ordination of a student signifies transference.... The gesture signifies a transfer or office...and of some graces (e.g., wisdom) by which the tasks connected with that office may be fulfilled" (99). In reviewing the laying-on of hands as it was highlighted in the Old Testament and early Christian literature, one is left with two major themes, identification and transference. There was a hint of laying-on of hands being utilized for healing, but as previously acknowledged, the practice could not be directly substantiated in the Old Testament. However, laying-on of hands for healing was pervasive in the New Testament and the ministry of Jesus and his followers.

The New Testament

According to Kraiss, there were approximately forty references to the laying-on of hands in the New Testament. Tipei clarified that twenty-five were direct references to the laying-on of hands, but there were only four instances where the "terminus technicus" or specialized description "laying-on hands," emerged (Acts 8:18, 1 Tm 4:14; 2 Tm 1:6 and Heb 6:2). Apparently, there were several verbs used interchangeably to indicate touch. They included the Greek word *hapto*, utilized in two passages relating to healing (e.g., Mt 14:36; 9:21). The Greek word *krateo* was used and carried the notion of keeping or holding (Mt 9:25), and the word *epitithemi*, which means "to lay or take hold of" (Mk 5:23; 7:32). This word was used most frequently when Jesus used laying-on of hands to effect healing.

In the New Testament, there were four distinct instances that the laying-on of hands was utilized. They included healing, conferral of the Holy Spirit, ordination/commissioning, and blessing. The dominant use as indicated by Kraiss, and Tipei was for *healing*. This was clearly represented in the ministry of Jesus, who used the laying-on of hands as one of the ways to mediate healing. Tipei indicated:

> The laying-on of hands in connection with the healing activity of Jesus is [directly] mentioned eight times. In three places, the gesture is part of a request addressed to Jesus: Jairus pleads with Jesus to lay his hand on his daughter (Mk 5:23; Mt 9:18); a deaf and dumb man is brought to Jesus that he might lay his hand on him (Mk 7:32). It follows, then, that there are only five occasions when it is clearly reported that Jesus laid hands on the sick: on a few at Nazareth (Mk 6:5), twice on a blind man (first "on him" [Mk 8:23], and the second time "on his eyes" [v.25]), on many at Capernaum (Lk 4:40) and on a woman with a "spirit of infirmity (Lk 13:13)." (100)

Kraiss and others have noted that the infirm were not only healed from Jesus being the initiator and touching them but also touching his clothing resulted in healing. This was clearly shown in the story of the hemorrhaging woman in Mark 5:27 and by "those troubled by evil spirits . . . who tried to touch him because power was coming from him and healing them all" (Lk 6:18, 19 [NIV]). The former was indeed a very powerful story where Jesus actually asked the question in Mk 5:30 (NIV), "Who touched my clothes?" because "power had gone out from him."

Remus (1977, 17) in *Jesus As Healer* indicated that [in] "what is known of ancient medicine, Jesus as healer and the account of the hemorrhaging woman are seen to be not atypical." He noted that healing was attributed to others during the era of Jesus. For the Greeks, it was the Greek god of healing, Aesculapius, who was lauded by Aelius Aristides, an Athenian statesman. For the Romans, according to eye-witness accounts recorded by the Roman historian Tacitus (*Histories* 4.81), it was the emperor Vespasian.

Lalleman (1997) in *Tyndale Bulletin,* however, argued that the origin of healing through touch was a distinctively Jewish-Christian phenomenon. He noted that when the Gospels referenced healing through touch, healing was so *immediate* that it precluded any other type of intervention. He highlighted the fact that Greek and Hellenistic texts stressed healing in a manner that allowed for the intervention of magic or medicine. Moreover, he refuted the work of Otto Weinreich (*Antike Heilungswunder* 1909) and scholars after him who advanced the notion that healing through touch predated Christianity.

Additionally, Lalleman challenged the claims in texts (Tacitus, *Histories* 4.81; Dio Cassius 65:8; Suetonius, *Vespasianus* 7 [*De vita caesarum VIII*]) that the emperor Vespasian healed through mere touch and stressed his use of spittle to heal a blind man and the placement of his heel on a lame man to mediate healing. He concluded, "It is improbable that Greek or Hellenistic stories about healing by touch were taken over by the early church and attributed to Jesus" (360). Thus, he suggested that healing through touch was unique to the ministry of Jesus, who "broke the barriers of uncleanness reaching out to the sick and allowing them to touch him" (361).

V.D. Loos (1965), in *The Miracles of Jesus,* correctly asserted, "The gift of healing was ascribed to all kinds of 'divine men,' but that there is a fundamental difference between these miracle-workers and Jesus. *The healings performed by Jesus reveal that every healing is at bottom God's work;* it is a display of divine mercy" (293). Close examination of the literature concerning the purpose of Jesus' healings and the miracles where he utilized the laying-on of hands clearly demonstrated that Jesus by word and deed was distinct from any healer, either factual or mythological.

The Purpose of Jesus' Healings

Why Did Jesus Heal?

Remus maintained that the claim of various scholars who have argued that Jesus was distinct from the pagan healers of his day as evidenced by the Gospel writers' concept of the Greek word for "miracle" was unsubstantiated. However, Cecil Hargreaves (1964), in *The Miracles of Jesus*, countered with an excellent observation. He noted that when Jesus talked about the miraculous deeds he was empowered to do, he did not use the Greek word *"teras,"* which meant a marvel or a wonder; he used the word *dunmeis*, which is translated "powers" or "mighty works" (Mk 6:5). He also used the words: *semeia*, "signs," and *erga*, meaning "works" (Jn 2:11; 5:36). He further asserted, "These words have moral and spiritual association: they imply 'acts of compassion' and 'acts of the Kingdom,'" as distinct from mere marvels" (27).

C.J. Waters (2002) indicated that Jesus healed to help individuals comprehend the "Good News." While he recognized that healing played a pivotal role in the ministry of Jesus, he perceived it as "subservient" rather than "central" (373). Greater emphasis was placed on the reality and the authority of the kingdom of God. Jesus was a fulfillment of one of the messianic prophecies given in Isaiah 61:1-2. His preaching and teaching about God's kingdom preceded the miraculous and served to demonstrate the reality of God's reign. Jesus was not a celestial short-order cook who ordered healings at will; his healings were always connected to the mission found in Isaiah 61:1-2. In conclusion, Waters contrasted the purpose of Jesus' healings to a sign that hung outside of a Spiritualist Church, "Healing—Tuesday at 7:30 pm." He observed, "Those circumstances in which healing may occur have to do not merely with the need of the sick (worthy though that is) but with the meaning of the ministry" (374).

Dr. Ian G. Wallis (1992), in agreement with Waters, highlighted how the healings of Jesus represented the nearness of God's kingdom. He also saw the healing ministry of Jesus as a validation of his "pedigree." He commented, "His therapeutic activity is subsumed within a broader category of the miraculous and presented as evidence for his identity in relation to God's salvific initiatives as paralleled in Exodus 4:1; 14:31" (43).

Peder Borgen (1981) asserted that while it was evident that Jesus preached about the coming kingdom of God and that his mission was one of action as demonstrated by healing, Jesus challenged and corrected the viewpoint of sickness and disease. It was a popular belief in Judaism that all sickness was a result of divine displeasure and resulted from some transgression or evil of the afflicted person (Miller, 1991). However, Borgen posited, "The NT [New Testament] view of health embraces the whole person, including both physical health and a religious-ethical life in accordance with God's will. *Both forgiveness of sins and the curing of bodily sickness are therefore included in the concept of salvation*" (101). While it was acknowledged that sickness and disease originated with the fall of man and there was sometimes a correlation between sickness and sin, Jesus' ministry of healing demonstrated that He had absolute power over man's physical, emotional, and spiritual maladies. Jesus, through healing, revealed the tangible initiation of God's kingdom and "brought the good news of Jesus Christ in man's concrete situation, of which the body is an important part. Thus, God's word took effect in action, and then often in the form of the healing of disease" (102).

Loos contributed that Jesus was a worker of miracles who functioned as a Messiah, Prophet, and Priest. As Messiah, he was the spiritual Savior of all. As a prophet, he facilitated the revelation of God. Finally as priest, he was so viscerally moved with compassion by the sufferings of others that he not only healed them but also ultimately sacrificed his life for their full redemption. Similar to Waters, Wallis, and Borgen, Loos concurred that a major purpose of the healings was to announce the advancement of God's kingdom; however, he offered that there were other purposes as well. They included: proving his identity, arousing faith, displaying mercy, and serving as a sign (233).

John Paul Heil (1979) examined the healing activity of Jesus with a Matthean lens. The healings represented a fulfillment of prophesy as portrayed in Mt 8:16-17; 11:2-5; 12:15-21. He suggested, "Various statements in Matthew indicate that the healings and exorcisms of Jesus are also signs of the apocalyptic-eschatological end-time, of the breaking-in and presence of the kingdom of God, of the long-awaited time of salvation" (276). In the various healing miracles performed in Matthew, he introduced theological themes like christology, ecclesiology, soteriology, and faith. He maintained that the consequences of the miracles were salvific in that the notion of the kingdom of God appearing was personified in their own lives. Frequently, the end result was faith in Jesus as healer and Savior.

James Kallas (1961), in *The Significance of the Synoptic Miracles,* extended the premise that the purpose of the healing miracles was to announce the kingdom of God by including in his discussion the topic of exorcism, which represented a healing of the mind, and by expounding on the concept of the kingdom. He asserted that by performing healing miracles, Jesus depicted what the kingdom of God actually resembled. He maintained that God's kingdom would become fully evident when Satan's rule was annihilated. Hence, in the midst of his physical healings, Jesus also drove out spirits that had traumatized individuals. In so doing, he was animating a very powerful proclamation found in Mt 12:28 (KJV), "But if I cast out devils [demons] by the Spirit of God then the kingdom of God has come upon you." Thus, whenever demons were expelled, Satan's dominance over a life was broken.

Keith Warrington's (2000) work, *Jesus The Healer: Paradigm or Unique Phenomenon,* emphasized that the purpose of the healings and exorcisms in the ministry of Jesus was to announce the kingdom of God. Healing was one of the evidences of the kingdom of God; however, in Jesus' public ministry, healing was associated with the preaching of the gospel. Warrington posited that a major distinction between healing performed by Jesus and his disciples was that the goal of Jesus was to actually initiate the kingdom of God and authenticate his role as Messiah. While Warrington stressed the importance of the teachings and healings of Jesus, he espoused that "it is Jesus' mission that culminates in the Cross that is to be recognized as the interpretative grid for the accurate reading of his healings and exorcisms" (12).

George Johnston (1960) in his consideration of the purpose of Jesus' healing alluded to the advancement of "God's Kingdom of love exercising its powers through the Messiah to bless people" (27). Concerning Jesus' ministry, he offered, "The healing ministry illustrates the basic purpose of Jesus. He had come to seek and to save the lost, the troubled, and the spiritually listless (Mk 2:17; 10:45; Lk 19:10; Jn 10:10). Sinful men are described as "sick" souls, without implying that ill-health is due to sin (Jn 9:3)" (28). The other purpose of Jesus' healing ministry noted by Johnston was the forgiveness of sins. In referencing the story of the healing of the paralytic in Mk 2:3-12, although healing was not mediated through the laying-on of hands, Johnston aptly concluded, ". . . the proper work of the Son [is] to invite sinners to return to God the Father . . ." (29). Jesus performed two healings. First, he healed him spiritually by forgiving his sins; second, he healed him physically by telling him to pick up his mat and return home.

Inauguration/Advancement of God's Kingdom

In summarizing the purpose of why Jesus healed, a major and critical theme that has emerged is the inauguration/advancement of the kingdom of God. In biblical scholarship, there has been an on-going discussion concerning the meaning of the terminology "kingdom of God." Since it has been acknowledged already that Jesus was not the only one to whom healing was attributed, it has been essential to review the definition and the nature of the kingdom of God as it lends further insight into the purpose of Jesus' healing.

In the *New International Dictionary of Old Testament Theology & Exegesis* and the *New International Dictionary of New Testament Theology* (1989), the phrase, "kingdom of God," was defined in light of three words. These three words were used to represent "kingdom" in the Bible. In the Old Testament, the Hebrew word was *malkut*; in the Aramaic, it was *malkuta*. Both words had the connotation of reigning. In the New Testament, the Greek word was *basileia* and meant "territory." In all of the definitions, "the overwhelming majority of instances use[d] the term with dynamic force." It was noted how in rabbinic tradition, "kingdom" was spiritualized and perceived as a place in the hearts of individuals. For the early Jews, there was the perception that this kingdom would be a political one in which the rule of the Romans would be broken. However, it was acknowledged that in the book of Matthew, in referencing the term, "kingdom of God, the biblical goal [was] the manifest exercise of God's sovereignty, his 'reign' on earth and among men" (*Zondervan's Theological Dictionaries*, s.v. "kingdom of God").

G.R. Beasley-Murray (1992) acknowledged that the term reflected authority, power, sovereignty, and kingship. He borrowed a quote from Hobbs found in the *Oxford English Dictionary* in which Hobbs described monarchy as, "a form of government which if he limited it by the law, is called a Kingdom; if by his own will, tyranny" (19). Hence, according to Beasley-Murray, "Kingdom thus is viewed as the lawful exercise of royal power, as over against tyranny, the unjust use of such authority. That is in accord with its meaning in the Bible" (19). He reflected on the message of Jesus in Mark 1:14-15, which stated, "Jesus came proclaiming the good news of God and saying, 'The time has been completed and the kingdom of God has drawn near; repent and believe in the good news'" (20). He acknowledged that through the words and actions of Jesus, God's salvific work was inaugurated and would consummate in a changed world.

Mark Saucy (1996) observed that Jesus preached a gospel message concerning the good news of the kingdom of God, which provoked individuals to make decisions about his reign in their lives. However, he cautioned against using the miracles of Jesus as an exclusive indicator of the arrival of God's kingdom since the Bible explicitly stated in John 20:30-31 that miracles were used to stimulate belief in Jesus as the Christ and Son of God. He also indicated that the display of the miraculous did not always guarantee a relationship with God, as seen in Matthew 7:21-23 where Jesus warned that not all who performed miracles would enter into heaven. Saucy saw Jesus in his divine love declaring war on Satan's cosmic kingdom, which was evidenced by sickness, disease, and disorder. In his estimation, miracles indicated the physical dimension of the kingdom of God.

T. Hartley Hall (1975) asserted that the kingdom of God mentioned by both Jesus and John the Baptist was realized only in the presence and person of Jesus. When John preached about the Kingdom of God, "repentance was a necessary step to be taken in anticipation of the Kingdom" (65). He recognized that when Jesus finally arrived, "repentance was no longer a precondition of grace but the response to it…" (65). He finally cautioned, "The distinction is crucial for Christian proclamation. Apart from it, it's hardly possible that the Kingdom is coming can be perceived as good news" (65).

In the book review of *Kingdom of God* edited by Bruce Chilton, reviewer Richard H. Hiers (1986) commented that Chilton did not envision Jesus regarding the kingdom of God as a concept that could be apprehended in either time or space. Jesus, in his evaluation, saw the kingdom as a "self-revelation of a personal God 'come in strength'" (313). Carl Henry (1992, 45) added that the kingdom of God was displayed in the body of Christ through the "presence of Jesus Christ, its invisible head. It is present in the Holy Spirit's dynamic, transforming power in the lives of saints…who are united in deep love for God." He commented that Jesus' view of the kingdom of God required inner change as reflected in John 3:3-5 where Jesus challenged Nicodemus.

The inauguration/advancement of the kingdom of God represents a critical and decisive theme in establishing one of the key purposes of the healing ministry of Jesus. However, other themes emerged when the miracles where Jesus healed primarily through touch have been examined. Using the Bible as a primary text, the miracles where Jesus used touch to mediate healing have been summarized. When other nuances occurred in the healing besides touch, they have also been mentioned. To facilitate this discussion, these criteria have been utilized to review/frame empirical studies: identifying participants, addressing the problem, describing the procedure, highlighting key results, and determining a theme. The miracles have been discussed in historical order as they occurred during Jesus' ministry. It is noted that, while Tipei mentioned only eight instances where it was directly implied that Jesus used his hands to mediate healing, the examples utilized in the discussion of specific miracles include indirect references where Jesus used his hands to heal.

The Miracles of Jesus in Relationship to the Laying-On of Hands 13

What Did Jesus Do? (W.D.J.D.)

Jesus Heals Peter's Mother-in-law (Lk 4:38,39; Mt 8:14-15; Mk 1:29-31)

This healing included Jesus and Peter's mother-in-law and occurred in Capernaum. She was suffering from a high fever and Jesus was asked to help her. While Matthew 8:14-15 (NIV) recorded, "He touched her hand, and the fever left her...," Luke 4:38-39 (NIV) added another detail to indicate, "He rebuked the fever, and it left her." The healing was immediate, and she rose and began to serve Jesus and the others present. In *The Expositor's Bible Commentary* (Gaebelein 1998, n.p.), it is noted that "Matthew mentions her service, not to tell his readers that those touched by Jesus [always] become his servants, but to make it clear that the miracle was effective and instantaneous...Jesus' authority instantly accomplished what he wills."

Hargreaves commented that this fever could have been malaria, which was common in swampy parts of Galilee. At this time, fever was viewed as a disease and not a symptom. He noted that in the Jewish Talmud, this kind of fever was referred to as "a burning fever" and the antidote consisted of tying an iron knife with plaited hair to a thorn bush for several days. A formula was to be spoken and healing would result. However, Jesus did not resort to magical formulas; Hargreaves affirmed that Jesus healed this woman by "a gesture and a word of authority and power" (89).

Warrington drew attention to the fact that while rabbinic tradition prohibited the touching of those with fever, Jesus touched the woman and was not defiled. Rather, the defiled became whole. He clearly saw Jesus acting in power and authority. He mentioned Luke's usage of the word *epetimesen*, translated "rebuke," when he healed the woman of the fever. This same term was used in Luke 4:35 and Mark 1:25-41 when Jesus addressed an evil spirit that had tormented a man who was present in the synagogue where he was teaching. The words of Jesus demonstrated his authority to subjugate any force that was inconsistent with the advancement of the kingdom of God.

Graham H. Twelftree (1999), in his erudite study, *Jesus, The Miracle Worker* mentioned the use of the word "rebuke." Regarding the woman's suffering, like Warrington, he referenced the use of the word *sunexomene* in Luke 4:38, translated as "seized, tormented, shut up, or hard pressed." He paralleled it to Luke 22:63 where Jesus was held prisoner to indicate the notion of being held captive. His point was that in keeping with Jesus' healing ministry, this woman was a captive who needed to be freed. Moreover, he saw this healing as another "example of Jesus' Spirit-empowered ministry" (148).

The dominant sub-theme, which emerged from this miracle in which both laying-on of hands and the spoken word were utilized, was that Jesus was given tremendous power and authority. Authority in the Greek was *exousia*. Zondervan's *Theological Dictionaries* defined *exousia* (derived from *exesti*, "it is possible, permitted, allowed") as the "power to act, which is given as a right by the virtue of the position [held]. Such authority exists quite independently of whether it can be exercised in given circumstances." The *exousia* of Jesus in his healing ministry "announce[d] that the devil and the demons have been deprived of their power: the One who is sent by God had the authority to destroy the works of the devil and to snatch men from his rule" (*Zondervan's Theological*

Dictionaries, s.v. "authority"). *Thus, the dominant theme in this healing was that Jesus had the authority to heal diseases.* This was the *first* healing in which the laying-on of hands was used to mediate healing, and the recipient was clearly identified. Moreover, in touching someone defiled, Jesus did not become defiled.

The Miracles of Jesus in Relationship to the Forgiveness of Sin

Jesus Heals a Paralytic (Lk 5:18-1; Mt 9:2-7; Mk 2:3-12)

Although healing was not mediated by the touch of Jesus, this healing is included because it serves as an immediate response to Jesus' laying hands on the leper and thematically portrays his increasing authority. In addition, it connects physical healing, regardless of the method employed, to spiritual healing—a major facet in the inauguration of God's kingdom.

This healing took place in Capernaum and included Jesus and the paralytic. Others privy to this healing were the Pharisees and teachers of the Law, the friends of the paralytic, and a crowd of people who had gathered to hear Jesus. It is noteworthy that Luke 5:17 (NIV) records, "And the power of the Lord was present for him to heal the sick." In the *Expositor's Bible Commentary*, "the presence of the Lord's power to heal means that God himself was there" (Gaebelein 1998, n.p.). In the *Hebrew Greek Study Bible*, the word *dynamis,* refers to "the great power of God, His almighty energy" (Zodhiates, 1612). On the surface, it appears that a crippled man who was carried in by four friends was in need of physical healing. While the man's physical need seemed most urgent, Jesus determined his deeper need was spiritual.

Then friends lowered the man into the room, Jesus observed the faith of the men and immediately forgave the paralytic of his sins. The Pharisees and teachers of the Law thought it was blasphemous for Jesus to forgive sins, for they reasoned that only God could forgive sins. Since Jesus knew their thoughts, he queried them as to which was easier, to forgive sins or to say, "Get up and walk." Hence, to demonstrate that he had the authority to forgive sins on earth, he commanded the man to get up and go home. Immediately the man stood and praised God. The man was granted a spiritual healing by his sins being forgiven, and he was granted a physical healing. All in the room were amazed, and they praised God.

Loos commented that Jesus focused on what was most important—the forgiveness of sin. He noted that man's total restoration was not connected to physical health and feeling better. Total restoration occurred when both man's soul and body were participants in the kingdom of God. He quoted Markus Van Leeuwen, who stated that there is "an indissoluble connection between the spiritual goods and the temporary benefactions of the Kingdom which appeared in Jesus" (444).

Birger Gerhardsson (1979) alluded to the indirect theme of faith. However, he concurred with Loos that the most salient theme was the forgiveness of sins. He saw the healing having two stages. The first stage was the forgiveness of sins; the second stage was the physical healing. To verify that the man's sins had been forgiven, the physical healing occurred. He highlighted the fact that in the healing of the paralytic, "we have a specific interpretation of what Jesus' healing more precisely means" (76). He observed that it was specifically in the book of Matthew that the theme of the forgiveness of sin was highlighted. In referencing Matthew 1:21, he noted that a critical part of Jesus' mission was "to save his people from their sins" (77). He drew attention to how this salvation would be fully realized when he highlighted the Last Supper in Matthew 26:28. Jesus and his disciples were having Communion and, after drinking the wine that symbolized his blood, he declared, "This is my blood...which is poured out for many for the forgiveness of sins." Hence, the healing of the paralytic stressed not only physical and spiritual healing, but his mission that would culminate on the Cross.

A point emphasized in *The Expositor's Bible Commentary* is that, when Jesus forgave the paralytic, it was not because he was more sinful than others were. He did so to emphasize that ultimately the origin of suffering was connected to man's estrangement from the Creator. In quoting Schweizer, the writer concludes that "Jesus must call attention to the man's deepest need; otherwise, the testimony of the healing would remain nothing more than the story of a remarkable healing" (Gaebelein 1998, n.p.).

In this healing, the theme of faith has been obscured by a more *dominant theme: Jesus had the authority to forgive sins.* This authority in particular deeply angered the religious leaders. His proclamation of being able to forgive sins made him equal to God. It was undeniable that he performed great healings, but in their expectation of a Messiah, not even he had the capacity to forgive sins. Furthermore, forgiveness of sins was not expressed in the Talmud (Loos, 445).

Faith in Jesus

Jesus Heals a Hemorrhaging Woman (Lk 8:43-48; Mt 9:20-21; Mk 5:25-34)

This healing occurred in Capernaum and included Jesus and the hemorrhaging woman. Others present were Peter, Jairus, and the crowd. This woman was described as having a blood condition in which she had hemorrhaged for more than twelve years. Besides the debilitated state that the constant loss of blood would entail, her condition made her ritually unclean. According to the Law found in Leviticus 15:19-27, not only was the woman considered unclean, but anyone or anything that she touched would also become unclean. Therefore, this woman was forced to live in isolation, apart from both her family and society. By the time that Jesus encountered the woman, she had exhausted her resources under the care of various physicians.

Touch became the medium that facilitated her healing. However, Jesus did not reach out to touch her; she reached out and touched his garment. Jesus, recognizing that power had gone out from him, in Luke 8:45-46 (NIV) queried, "Who touched me? Someone touched me; I know that power has gone out from me." When the woman identified herself and told what happened, Jesus responded in Luke 8:48 (NIV), "Daughter, your faith has healed you. Go in peace." A consequence of this woman touching Jesus was that she was immediately healed. The Greek word for "healed" used in this context was *sozo*, and the tense implied that this healing "would continue to affect her life." While the initial healing was physical, *sozo* also implied soul salvation, giving the healing a soteriological slant. Thus, Jesus sent her away in peace (Twelftree, Warrington).

It is worth noting that when Jesus asked who had touched him, he used the Greek word for touch, *hapato*. In the *Hebrew-Greek Study Bible*, *hapto* "implies a certain degree of involvement with the object on the part of the subject, more than mere contact or touch, [it implies] an engagement, handling, or use in which some kind of influence or effect is created between the items coming into contact" (Zodhiates, 1592). In touch, there was a *transmission of power*.

Jesus used the word "power" to describe what flowed from him. The Greek word for power previously mentioned was *dynamis*, suggesting power, might, strength, force, ability, capability, deed of power, and resources (Gaebelein 1998, n.p.). It is interesting to observe that the word *energeia*, which is Greek for "energy," is a synonym of *dynamis* and referred to "activity, operation, or working. It was power in operation; the expending of energy in an effort or undertaking" (Zodhiates, 1612). Warrington noted that while some commentators saw the woman's behavior in touching his garment "border[ing] on a quasi-magical or superstitious act" (65), Jesus regarded it as an act of faith. Tipei added, Jesus' power is not "mana which can be . . . discharged at a simple involuntary touch" (103). He maintained that Jesus was empowered by the *Holy Spirit* to heal.

Regarding the faith of the woman, Twelftree noted that healing the woman could not be based on psychosomatic (mind over matter) beliefs. It had to be based on faith and trust that was receptive to the power of Jesus. It was a faith that would not only bring physical healing but also have theological implications (157). Thus, she was addressed as "daughter." Hence, even when Jesus commanded her to go in peace, "it means not just freedom from inward anxiety, but that *wholeness* or *completeness* of life that comes from being brought into a right relationship with God" (Gaebelein 1989, n.p.). Hargreaves pointed out how persevering faith was critical in this woman's healing. Larry Richards (1998) noted that the woman was healed because she expressed faith in Jesus; it was not attached to any personal merit.

Once again, there is the underlying theme of someone disenfranchised being restored physically, spiritually, emotionally, and socially. Marla Selvidge (1984) observed, "The miracle story about the woman with the "flow of blood" subtly shatters the legal purity system and its restrictive social conditioning" (622). Keathley added, "Jesus touches unclean people [to] illustrate the doing away with the law and the whole idea of ritual uncleanness. Something new was happening and Jesus accepts all people who believe in Him no matter what their status in society" (16). While the woman was cognizant of the fact that many were healed by the touch of Jesus, it was not "touch" which catalyzed her miracle. It was faith in the one she touched that effected the change. Therefore, the *dominant theme stressed in this healing is the importance of faith in Jesus.*

Authority Over Death

The Healing of Jarius' Daughter (Mk 5:21-43; Mt 9:18-26; Lk 8:40-56)

The healing occurred in Capernaum and included Jesus, Jairus, and Jarius' daughter. Others present and privy to the miracle were her mother, Peter, James, and John. Professional mourners and a crowd had gathered, but Jesus dismissed them. Jairus was a ruler in the synagogue who had a daughter who was initially very sick. When Jairus first approached Jesus, he begged Jesus to come and place his hands on her so she could be healed. However, on the way to his house, Jesus encountered the woman with the issue of blood. During the time that Jesus was healing her, word was brought to Jairus that his daughter had died and that he should no longer bother the teacher. However, Jesus addressed Jairus and admonished him not to be afraid but to believe. Upon reaching the house, Jesus encountered noisy mourners. He told them that the girl was not dead but asleep. They laughed at him, and he put them out of the house. With only her parents and the disciples present, Jesus took the girl by the hand and said to her in Mark 5:41 (NIV), "*Talitha koum!* Little girl, I say to you, get up!" Luke 8:55-56 (NIV) records, "Her spirit returned, and at once she stood up. Then Jesus told them to give her something to eat." Her parents were amazed, and Jesus ordered them not to tell anyone. However, the news of this healing spread quickly throughout the entire region. It is noted that in the account given in Matthew 9:18-26, the girl has just died and Jairus asked Jesus to put his hands on her to bring her back to life.

Warrington noted the reoccurring instances where Jesus performed a miracle that should have made him ritually unclean—touching a corpse. However, in the demonstration of his authority, He reanimated the corpse. He stressed the faith of the father who believed that Jesus could bring his dead daughter back to life.

Keathley stressed the compassion of Jesus who told the mourners not to cry. He also highlighted the veracity of Jesus' statement when he told the mourners that she was only asleep, noting that Jesus knew that "sleep is a euphemism for temporal death" (17). He saw the resurrection again as demonstrating the deity of Christ and validating his messianic claims. Finally, he observed that God was given more glory because a dead child was resurrected.

Jairus was a man of faith who believed that the touch of Jesus could bring his daughter back to life. That was why he sought him. Even Jesus told Jairus to believe. However, it was not the faith of Jairus that brought his daughter back to life; it served as a catalyst. It was ultimately the authority of Jesus over death that accomplished this miracle. Thus, while having some significance, the critical theme in this miracle is not faith or method. The dominant theme is Jesus' display of his authority over death through his words.

Jesus Heals a Deaf Man

Jesus Heals a Hearing and Speech-Impaired Man (Mk 7:31-37)
This healing took place in the region of Decapolis and included Jesus and a hearing-and speech-impaired man. Others present were the friends who brought the man to Jesus; however, they did not witness the actual miracle. Friends brought a hearing-and speech-impaired man to Jesus and begged Jesus to lay his hands on the man to bring about healing. Jesus took the man away from the crowd. He placed his fingers in the man's ears; he spit and touched the man's tongue. Finally, he looked up to heaven, sighed, and spoke, "Be opened." The man's ears were opened and his tongue was "loosened" immediately. His speech was clear. Again, there was an injunction for silence. However, his request was not heeded. Because of this healing, the people were "overwhelmed" and their response in Mark 7:37 (NIV) was, "He has done everything well... He makes the deaf hear and the mute speak." The news of this healing spread rapidly in an area that was primarily Gentile.

Loos noted that while the man's friends specifically asked Jesus to lay his hands on him, Jesus responded with a variety of gestures. He observed that little was known of this man or the nature of his illness. While some believed that man had some facility of speech, others posited that his sickness might have been deaf-mutism, which would have rendered him unable to speak. He noted the "sighing" of Jesus and the "looking up to heaven" as his way of communicating with his Father. He did not interpret his behavior as a part of the modus operandi. He concluded that if Jesus would have required his gestures as part of a formula for doing miracles, it would have been duplicated in early Christianity. However, the only condition that was required when healing was done was to ask "in the name of Jesus" (327).

In addition to the sighing and looking up to heaven, Jesus added other elements to this healing. Was he ignoring the request of the men? Was he suggesting another way of healing? John Calvin (1979) in *Commentary on a Harmony of the Evangelists* offered this insight:

> The laying-on of hands would of itself have been sufficiently efficacious, and even, without moving a finger, he might have accomplished it by a single act of his will, but it is evident that he made abundant use of outward signs, when they were found to be advantageous. Thus, by touching the tongue with spittle, he intended to point out that the faculty of speech was communicated by himself alone.... By putting his fingers into the ears, he showed that it belonged to his office to pierce the ears of the deaf. (271–272)

All that Jesus did in word or deed was connected to a particular purpose. It is worth noting that the Greek word used to describe the man's speech was *mogilalos*, which implied being tongue-tied, hardly talking, or having a speech impediment (Gaebelein 1998, n.p.). This rare word was used only once in the New Testament. However, it was reflected in Isaiah 35:5-6 (NIV) that prophetically spoke of a Messianic age in which "the ears of the deaf were unstopped...and the mute tongue shouted for joy." Hence, in this healing, the specificity of Jesus placing his fingers in the man's ears and touching his tongue *thematically suggests fulfillment of a Messianic Proclamation*. This theme is very much in keeping with the initiation of the kingdom of God. Isaiah 35:5-6 declared that in the messianic age those who could not see, hear, walk, or speak would be healed.

Jesus Heals a Man Blind Since Birth (Jn 9)

This healing included Jesus and a blind man and happened in Jerusalem. Others present included the disciples. Jesus and his disciples were walking in Jerusalem; they encountered a man who suffered from congenital blindness. The disciples queried Jesus as to who had sinned to cause this man's blindness. Jesus responded that no one had sinned and affirmed that the purpose of the man's blindness was to display the work of God in his life. Having spoken, Jesus spit on the ground and made mud with the saliva. Using his hands, he placed the mud on the man's eyes. He then instructed the man to go and wash in the Pool of Siloam.

After following the instruction of Jesus, the man was healed. Outside of his physical healing, the man, when questioned by Jesus about his belief in the Son of God, experienced a second healing. Initially, the man did not know that Jesus was the Son of God, but his response in John 9:36, "Who is he, sir? Tell me so that I may believe in him," indicated a desire for spiritual awakening. In discovering that he was in the presence of Jesus, he confessed his belief and worshipped him. Worship, which is *proskyneo* in the Greek, highlighted the image of "paying reverence and homage to deity" and "rendering divine honors" (Zodhiates, 1669). Thus, his response to his healing was to worship and follow Jesus.

The Expositor's Bible Commentary has emphasized the fact that while Jesus had healed others who were blind, this was the first example of healing congenital blindness. Rather than bringing restoration or remediation of sight, he had to perform a "creative" miracle rather than a "remedial" one (Gaebelein 1998, n.p.). Barnabas Lindar (1981), in his commentary *The Gospel of John,* suggested that Jesus made clay from the mud and his saliva to resemble the creation of man from the dust in Genesis 2:7.

Interesting to observe that in John 9:5 (NIV) Jesus declared, "I am the light of the world." This miracle further established that as the "light of the world," Jesus' goal in performing this miracle was connected again to his kingdom mission of bringing the good news of Christ to a world that was spiritually blind (Twelftree, 1999; Warrington, 2000). This pattern of blindness was further conveyed when the Pharisees found out about the miracle. While they were willing to admit that God should be given glory for the miracle, they flatly rejected Jesus. Hence, in John 9:39 (NIV) he intimated, "I have come into this world so that the blind would see and those who see will become blind." The Pharisees were insulted by Jesus' comment. They assumed that they could "see without his intervention" (Gaebelein 1998, n.p.). However, Jesus' response to them was one of censure. He recognized that they were blind in that they refused to acknowledge that he brought light to their spiritual darkness. Consequently, in their rejection of him, they would stay bound by their sins and suffer judgment.

In this healing, once more, Jesus used his hands to facilitate the miraculous. Yet, the only command spoken was when Jesus instructed the man to go and wash in the Pool of Siloam. Jesus did not place emphasis on how he healed, but he used this opportunity to demonstrate four critical points. First, he reiterated afresh that the purpose of healing was to glorify God. Second, he stressed the importance of salvific faith and obedience. Third, he underscored his soteriological function as the "Light of the World." Fourth, he identified with precision the increasing spiritual blindness of those who purported to see. *Therefore, the dominant theme to emerge from this miracle is that Jesus' authority to heal was indelibly associated with soul salvation.* For in this miracle, the man did not ask to be healed, nor did friends bring him to Jesus. Jesus of his own volition initiated the man's physical healing and then sought him out to offer spiritual healing. Twelftree offered, "He require[d] no one to direct or guide him in his ministry, save his Father" (213).

Jesus Heals a Woman Bound by Satan (Lk 13:10-17)

This miracle included Jesus and a crippled woman. It took place in Jerusalem or Galilee. Others present were the ruler of the synagogue and the multitude in attendance. Jesus was teaching in a synagogue and noticed a woman who had been crippled by a spirit for eighteen years. This illness left her unable to stand up straight. Without a request from her, Jesus called to her and told her that she was freed (v.12) from her infirmity. Next, he placed his hands on her, and she immediately stood straight. Her response to this healing was to praise God. However, a synagogue leader took issue with Jesus for healing the woman on the Sabbath. Jesus accused him of being a hypocrite because he knew that this religious leader would untie his ox or donkey to give it water on the Sabbath. Hence, he stressed in Luke 13:16 (NIV), "This woman, a daughter of Abraham whom Satan has kept bound for eighteen long years [should] be set free on the Sabbath day from what bound her." The religious leader was humiliated, but the people rejoiced about the miraculous things that Jesus was doing.

Loos highlighted that some have suggested that the woman may have suffered from scoliosis, hysterical curvature of the spine, or a contracture of the second cervical vertebra. This condition would bring mental as well as physical anguish. He emphasized that Jesus wanted to make it clear that he was in fact Lord over the Sabbath, and he wanted to point out the hypocrisy of the leader. In healing her in the synagogue, he showed that the needs of people were more important than the legalistic keeping of the Law. He noted that Jesus ascribed her condition to the workings of a supernatural malevolent force and summarily liberated her from it (520-522).

In addition, *The Expositor's Bible Commentary* indicated that it was evident that she was spirit oppressed and not possessed, for there was no reference in the Gospels to suggest that Jesus ever touched anyone that was demon possessed: "Far more important, and emphasized by Luke, was the woman's instant healing and its direct attribution to God. This of course showed that Jesus was truly acting with God's authority" (Gaebelein 1998, n.p.).

Concurring with Loos, Hargreaves noted how Jesus dismissed the ruler of the synagogue, "a stubborn upholder of Jewish orthodoxy…who was obviously missing completely the meaning of Jesus teaching about the kingdom" (183). A consequence of the preaching about the *kingdom of God was the liberation of those held captive*. He observed yet another example where Jesus took the initiative to bring about healing. Faith was not the issue, nor was his behavior in response to a particular request. In referencing the Sabbath, he offered that Jesus did not violate the Sabbath; he amended some of the rules, which often disregarded the needs of people. Hargreaves recognized that this was Jesus' last appearance in the synagogue. In bringing joy to many, he had angered the religious elite. In Luke's Gospel, it was clear that Jesus was now in route to Jerusalem where he would suffer and die on the cross.

Warrington not only drew attention to the fact that Jesus was reinterpreting the purpose of the Sabbath by healing the woman on this day but also addressed the attitude of Jesus' opponent, the religious leaders. He commented, "[They] are embarrassingly blind to their loveless reliance on dogma. Instead of rejoicing, . . . they are outraged because Jesus has broken the rules that they perceive to determine correct behavior for a Sabbath. While recognizing his capacity to heal, . . . they fail to see his authority over the Sabbath" (117). He added that some of the anger expressed by his this leader resulted not only from his hypocrisy being exposed but also from the lack of spiritual understanding concerning the Sabbath. The leader's latent pride as part of the religious elite blinded him to the truth that Jesus sought to impart.

A verbal command and the laying-on of hands mediated another healing. However, the procedure was not accentuated. What was most critical was the issue of the Sabbath. The point was that Jesus in Matthew 12:8 (NIV) had already declared, "For the Son of Man is Lord of the Sabbath." Hence, the cause of disagreement was his messianic claims and the *exsousia* or power he displayed. The fact that Jesus did not spend time addressing those he healed on the Sabbath but generally directed his attention to the religious leaders demonstrates that in performing these healings, outside of any compassion he may have felt for their plight, he was confronting the hypocritical leaders with the truth. He was the Messiah sent by God with tremendous power and authority. Thus, while the laying-on of hands was used to mediate the healing, *the major theme is that Jesus had authority over the Sabbath*. Ultimately, all of the healings, which validated his authority, also paved the way for his death.

Connecting the Dots

In summarizing Jesus' use of the *laying-on of hands* for healing, it is evident that Jesus healed through touch. However, while the practice of touch reflected how some healings were mediated in antiquity, Jesus' healings were purposeful in that they demonstrated a divine transfer of power, caring to the recipient, and messianic fulfillment. As already indicated, Jesus was not limited to any particular method. Sometimes Jesus touched and spoke; sometimes he used saliva and mud. However, frequently, Jesus used his word to effect healing. He told his disciples in Mark 16:18 that when they laid hands on the sick, they would recover; however, the emphasis in the healing was never placed on method.

In the ministry of Jesus, healing was connected to his divine purpose, which was to inaugurate the kingdom of God. As a demonstration of the kingdom's advance, physical healings served as only one of the messianic signs. The more critical emphasis in the advancement of the kingdom was placed on the preaching of the good news of Christ who brought spiritual healing to a world separated from God by sin. Thus, outside of healing, most of Jesus' time was spent teaching about salvation. Moreover, John the Baptist, who served as the forerunner to Jesus, spent most of his time preaching repentance. *The preaching of repentance was not to prepare people for physical healing; it was done as a prerequisite to open hearts to Jesus' message of salvation.*

In the examination of the miracles where touch was employed, salient themes have emerged to display Jesus' increasing *exousia*, which culminated on the cross. The key themes include: authority to heal disease, authority to restore the disenfranchised, authority to forgive sins, authority over death, authority to fulfill messianic proclamations, and authority over the Sabbath. Other themes indicate that the authority to heal was connected to soul salvation, grace and mercy, faith, and the gradualism of spiritual discernment.

In summarizing the history of Christian-based laying-on of hands, the sagacious observations of two men have been noted. First, O'Mathuna (2001) commented:

> The biblical laying-on of hands is a complex symbol and ritual soaked with religious meaning. Central to it is the belief that the power of God is being called upon to witness and empower an event, be it commissioning or a healing. The laying-on of hands was never seen as a healing technique to

be used apart from the power of God. Only his choice would bring about healing, not the will of the patient or healer. The one laying-on hands was not believed to be tapping into an impersonal energy accessible by all. (37)

One premise of the research has been that Jesus as a healer was unique in both his purpose and mission. While it has been maintained that the laying-on of hands was one way in which healing was mediated, it has been established that Jesus was not dependent or this or any other method. Second, Morton T. Kelsey (1995) offered:

> Jesus was not concerned with a mechanical spirituality, to be used as one follows the textbook laws of physics or mathematics. Such a conception of reality is far from the mind and attitude of Jesus. His was to bring people into a faith relationship to the loving God by the various methods of touching, speaking commands, compassion, and forgiveness, so that the power of the living God might be more fully in touch with them and restore them. Then he set about teaching them. (69)

In Christendom when authentic healing took place, the end result was not simply physical healing. Jesus demonstrated in his life and ministry that the purpose of healing was to *bring those in need of spiritual healing into relationship with his Father*. For this reason, he confronted those who sought healing with the truth of man's plight. As Savior, he offered himself as God's remedy. Against the backdrop of eternity, *spiritual healing* took precedence over physical healing. Thus, the litmus test for any group or individual today that promotes healing is not necessarily whether lives are replete with the outpouring of the miraculous and physical health is restored. The more critical issue is if those individuals who experience healing have been brought into a growing relationship with the Father through repentance and discipleship. There lies the crux of Jesus' healing, regardless of the method used. Jesus' healing resulted in physical and spiritual transformation. It drew individuals back to God. Since Reiki practitioners claim to have used the same method and have had access to the same "divine energy," it is from the template of Scripture and biblical Jesus that the claims of Reiki practitioners have been examined.

A Biblical Worldview 14

Now having specifically discussed Christ-based healing as it is reflected in the Bible and as it is practiced today, we turn our attention to understanding a biblical worldview. In chapter 6, we explored the pantheistic worldview that encompasses Reiki healing. Not only was there no distinction between the created and the Creator, but "reality" or "God" was perceived as an omnipresent but impersonal force that could not be known. In the discussion of theism, the religions of Christianity, Judaism, and Islam are highlighted. In each of these religions' view of reality, a personal God who exists creates a finite universe. Reality is both material and spiritual. Human beings are perceived as individuals who are created in God's image. They are external, physical, and spiritual beings. Their perception of truth is that it emanates from God. God allows humankind to be informed via revelation about the physical world through reason, sense, and experience. It should be noted that while revelation can be mediated through creation, God is responsible for clarifying the content in revelation. In addition, an individual does not know all truth; however, God knows all truth. In terms of values, there is an objective reality. One's moral template is formulated by the boundaries of a sovereign God.

Relational Theism

Although Judaism, Christianity, and Islam are included in the broad rubric of monotheism, there is a major difference that cannot be reconciled. Thus, there are terms used today like "relational theism," "Christian theism," or a "biblical worldview" to highlight the distinctiveness of God discussed in the Bible. In Islam, Judaism, and some branches of Christianity that are often referred to as cults, the role of Jesus is minimized or left out completely. While hailed as a teacher, prophet, and even "Son of God," Jesus is not considered God. Yet, there can be no real discussion about the healing specifically talked about in the Bible without acknowledging Jesus as God. When healing was discussed in the Old Testament, it was clear that the source of the healing was God. In the New Testament, the source of healing is still God. However, it is mediated through the ministry of Jesus and later the ministry of the Holy Spirit. Although there are many accounts of Jesus using hands-on healing, or speaking the Word of God to bring about healing, those miraculous signs were performed primarily to demonstrate the presence of God's kingdom as well as to fulfill Messianic prophecies and demonstrate that Jesus was who he said He was. Consequently, the greatest healing to take place was the healing of the spirit or salvation.

Jesus was sent to repair the broken fellowship that existed between sinful man and a holy God. Hence, the emphasis on healing was also very relational. Not everyone who sought out physical or emotional healing was desirous of a personal relationship with God through accepting Jesus' offer of forgiveness. However, the invitation was extended to those who wanted it. In both Islam and Judaism, one encounters a God who is sovereign, transcendent, moral, righteous, omniscient, benevolent, and wise. What is missing in both instances is the presence of a Savior to pay the price for the fullness of salvation, body, soul and spirit. In John (1:14), the Bible records how "the Word became flesh and dwelt among us...." Of course, the "Word" was Jesus. James Sire (2009), in *The Universe Next Door,* correctly observes, "The main point for us is that theism declares that God can and has clearly communicated with us. Because of this we can know much about who God is and what he desires for us" (147).

Seven Worldview Questions

In Davis' (2007) article entitled, "What is Theism?" he provides answers to the 7 worldview questions as they relate to theism.

1. What is the nature of Ultimate Reality (God)? There is a sovereign, infinite, and transcendent God who creates and sustains the universe.

2. What is the nature of material reality (the world and everything in it)? The material world was not an accident in the cosmos. It was planned and created by God.

3. What is humanity? Humans were created by God in his image.

4. What happens to a person at death? When humans die, they are judged by God and spend eternity with or away from him.

5. Why is it possible to know anything at all? God has created human beings with intellect and the ability to obtain information.

6. How do we know what is right or wrong? God has given a moral code and has revealed what is right and wrong through Scripture.

7. What is the meaning of human history? History is linear. It was created by God and all things are moving towards God's plan of completion.

In the Words of a Biblical Theist

In biblical theism, the emphasis is always placed on the Creator. While there is a celebration about His "works," there is a clear distinction between the created and the Creator. There is also a desire to take direction and live a life that is pleasing to God. Rather than an unknowable force or even a transcendent God that cannot be reached, this God is personal and sought daily. In Psalm 19 (Message), David expresses the sentiment of a consummate biblical theist.

> [1-2] *God's glory is on tour in the skies, God-craft on exhibit across the horizon. Madame Day holds classes every morning, Professor Night lectures each evening.* [3-4] *Their words aren't heard, their voices aren't recorded, But their silence fills the earth: unspoken truth is spoken everywhere.* [4-5] *God makes a huge dome for the sun—a superdome! The morning sun's a new husband leaping from his honeymoon bed, The day breaking sun, an athlete racing to the tape.* [6] *That's how God's Word vaults across the skies from sunrise to sunset, Melting ice, scorching deserts, warming hearts to faith. The revelation of* GOD *is whole and pulls our lives together. The signposts of* GOD *are clear and point out the right road. The life-maps of* GOD *are right, showing the way to joy. The directions of* GOD *are plain and easy on the eyes.* GOD's *reputation is twenty-four carat gold, with a lifetime guarantee. The decisions of* GOD *are accurate down to the nth degree.* [10] *God's Word is better than a diamond, better than a diamond set between emeralds. You'll like it better than strawberries in spring, better than red, ripe strawberries.* [11-14] *There's more: God's Word warns us of danger and directs us to hidden treasure. Otherwise how will we find our way? Or know when we play the fool? Clean the slate, God, so we can start the day fresh! Keep me from stupid sins, from thinking I can take over your work; Then I can start this day sun-washed, scrubbed clean of the grime of sin. These are the words in my mouth; these are what I chew on and pray. Accept them when I place them on the morning altar, O God, my Altar-Rock, God, Priest-of-My-Altar.*

Part Three

You Shall Know Them by their Fruit

The Myth of Reiki Safety 15

One of the pleas of David in Psalm 19 was, "[God] Keep me from stupid sins, from thinking I can take over your work." True healing is God's work. However, those who practice Reiki and other energy-based modalities have erroneously concluded that they are able to "heal on demand without" any side effects or consequences. Some in the medical community have dismissed Reiki since "...the evidence is *insufficient* to suggest that [R]eiki is an effective treatment for any condition," (Lee, Pittler, and Ernst, 2008). However, just because something is dismissed because its effectiveness has not been proven does not dismiss the fact that the practice can be harmful. Although suggestions have been made about examining the safety of Reiki, most studies are more concerned about it's effectiveness than Reiki having any *harmful side effects*.

Reiki Web of Safety

Kelner et al. (2002) in their study, which examined the views of practitioners of Reiki concerning safety, maintained that Reiki practitioners felt it was safe. Again, they felt they needed nothing to support that claim. Words and phrases such as "non-invasive," "gentle laying-on of hands," "transference of energy," and "could do no harm," punctuated the discussion. One practitioner, however, offered that Reiki sometimes activated an emotional response. Nevertheless, "in spite of this concern, the need for scientific proof of safety was not salient to this group" (237). Gallob, Nield-Anderson and Ameling, and Mansour et. al emphasized Reiki's apparent "unobtrusive," "non-invasive," and "harmless" nature. Kennedy strongly emphasized that "Reiki was not a threat to medicine but an asset," (7), while Wardell and Engebretson (2001) indicated, 'Touch therapies [like Reiki] remain a very low risk, low cost intervention, and within the scope of the nursing practice" (444).

Miles, in "Reiki Vibrational Healing," gave a somewhat complex response when asked the question, "How can Reiki help if it can't harm?" She maintained that the help/harm model was reflective of "dualistic" patterns of thought. She offered that unlike allopathic (western) medicine where patients were being physically engaged by medical practitioners, in Reiki, the alleged energy field was accessed. Thus, there was no real medical involvement. Therefore, "[Reiki] doesn't have to have the power to harm in order to help. The help/harm duality is true when we are talking about surgery or drugs which function unidirectionally, but Reiki is a vibrational modulator" (82). Since research showed high blood levels and blood urea levels dropping with Reiki, Miles surmised, "It could be evidence that Reiki functions as a modulator (something that makes changes) which means the harm/health duality is not operative" (82).

Reiki Contraindications—Warnings from Literature

As comforting as her theory may sound, words, such as "low risk" and "triggering an emotional response," indicate a need for some caution. Moreover, O'Mathuna (2001) in his research on Human Energy Field Therapies, another category that included Reiki, issued a grave warning from a medical doctor who had personal experience with life energies. In directly quoting the physician, O'Mathuna warned, "Tapping these energies is fire, and the consequences are serious and can be dangerous.... The consequences of immature judgment, of toying with the chakra system, can be psychosis, aggravation of neuroses, acceleration of disease processes and suicide" (118).

In an obscure monograph, generally not available in the United States and never mentioned or endorsed as a text read by Reiki practitioners, David Ashworth (2001), in *Dancing with the Devil: Survival for Healers and Therapists,* convincingly chronicled his personal experiences with Reiki and shared case histories of clients that he counseled. Although openly admitting his involvement in the occult, he added a level of candor not normally found in Reiki literature. In talking about Reiki energy, he wrote:

> We say [Reiki] has its own consciousness. This is a judgment made from experience: we know it goes where it is supposed to when we use it in a healing situation, but we don't really know its source.... Nobody knows for sure. For all we know it could be one of Satan's immaculate deceptions. The truth is, we don't know where it comes from.... We work from a center of love and bring into our being light which we perceive as from a divine source. The work we do with this ... energy achieves results, which benefit those whom we are trying to help, but ... we cannot say for certain that we know what we are connecting with and what we are bringing through our system.... Reiki opens you up! We are opening doors and we can access things accidentally that can cause us a great deal of anxiety, pain and discomfort. (47–49)

As previously mentioned, Ashworth was a practitioner of Reiki; nevertheless, in his book, he went to great lengths to describe possible side effects. While one could take issue with his belief that practitioners can protect themselves, he still took responsibility in asserting that Reiki could cause harm to both the recipient and practitioner.

Whitsitt's (1988) article entitled, "Reiki Therapy" in the *Journal of Christian Nursing,* represented the *only* entry in any published journal that spoke out against the practice of Reiki. In describing Reiki energy, he alluded to a telephone interview with a "Reiki therapist/Tarot card consultant" who maintained, "Reiki balances and clears the chakra system" (12). He mentioned the psycho-spiritual dangers alluded to in Hindu culture when the alleged "chakra powers" were activated and the *kundalini* force, in the form of a snake, arose. The force "represented at the base of the spine by the Hindu god, Shakti, …ascends to the seventh chakras and unites with Shiva, the third member of the Hindu trinity"(12-13). This process, possibly triggered by the laying-on of hands in Reiki, opened a person up to psychic experiences. He offered that there were Reiki masters who channeled spirit guides to facilitate the "pseudo-healing sessions" (13). Using the Bible as his point of reference, he argued from Deuteronomy 18:9-12 and Acts 16:16-18 and condemned Reiki as an occult practice.

While many practitioners of Reiki would be dismissive of biblical standards that they interpret as dogmatic and narrow, Whitsitt's view is important in that it represents the sentiments of a vast majority of spiritually discerning, Bible-believing Christians towards any activity with occult associations, and his view signals both spiritual and psychological dangers.

In the article, "Spiritual Side Effects," Maricris Briones (2002) quoted physician Terry Ruhl in his April 22 letter to the *Archives of Internal Medicine*. Ruhl commented, "One should not introduce a therapeutic method with spiritual implications to a religious patient without informing the patient of potential conflicts…. Since patients are often unaware of the spiritual philosophies behind their treatment, *they should be informed*"(1). Briones further posited, "Informed medical consent—designed to help patients make good decisions about proceeding with or refusing a course of medical treatment—is more than an ethical quandary. It's also a legal obligation" (1).

Without informing patients of Reiki's spiritual moorings, approval in hospital settings had the possibility of convincing unsuspecting patients that the practice of Reiki was safe because it was being administered in a medical environment. While there may be anecdotal stories about the short-term salubrious effects of Reiki in these settings, patients have been placing themselves in spiritual peril although they may initially "feel" better. In allopathic medicine, it is acknowledged that a prescribed medication may have some side effects, and the patient is informed. No such contraindication is given as it relates to Reiki. Reiki is not a non-invasive, non-sectarian scientific practice. It is a spiritual practice with side effects, these effects are often manifested in time. An outspoken supporter of Reiki, Reiki-Master William Rand made a telling personal comment concerning Reiki: "My own parents are born-again Christians. They don't want Reiki, and I would never give it to them." The question is "why?" Perhaps, they are instinctively discerning what others are now recognizing.

The Catholic Church Speaks Out

After receiving numerous questions concerning the Catholic Church's position on the use of Reiki, the United States Conference of Catholic Bishops presented a paper in March of 2009, entitled *Guidelines for Evaluating Reiki as an Alternative Therapy*. They concluded the following. They stated:

> Reiki therapy finds no support either in the findings of natural science or in Christian belief. For a Catholic to believe in Reiki therapy presents insoluble problems. In terms of caring for one's physical health or the health of others, to employ a technique that has no scientific support (or even plausibility) is generally not prudent.

In terms of caring for one's spiritual health, there are important dangers. To use Reiki, one would have to accept at least in an implicit way, central elements of the worldview that undergirds Reiki theory, elements that belong neither to Christian faith nor to natural science. (5-6 retrieved 3/8/10)

They recognized that the worldview that supported Reiki belonged to religions from the East and possessed a "...certain monistic and pantheistic character...." (5) They also noted that some practitioners of Reiki spoke of being in contact with "angelic beings" or "spirit guides" that could subject those involved with Reiki to "...further danger of exposure to malevolent forces or powers." (6) Another concern was that of superstition and idolatry which would ultimately lead individuals away from worship of God. Although the use of Reiki was banned from being used at Catholic institutions, some practitioners scoffed at the idea of the Catholic Church dictating morality and claimed that they had not named specific studies in their report.

Lauie Lumby Schmidt (2009), a Catholic spiritual director, Reiki Master, and writer in her article, *Reiki Allows Me To Continue The Healing Ministry of Jesus*, chooses to disregard the warnings. After using Reiki on a grief-stricken woman who also suffered from Multiple Sclerosis, the woman intimated, "The pain of the grief and the loss have simply melted away. I feel like I have been resting within a warm vessel of peace and love." Convinced by this woman's positive experience, Schmidt wrote:

> Regardless of the limitations some might perceive within the philosophy or practice of Reiki, this incident proved to me, beyond a doubt, that Reiki can be a powerful tool through which God facilitates healing. No one can convince tell me otherwise.
> It is for this reason that in spite of the prohibitions set forth by a U.S. Bishops committee, I continue to openly share Reiki. While some might accuse me of disobedience, I am content in knowing that to God, the ultimate Authority, my obedience is true.
> As a Reiki practitioner and instructor of "Christ-centered hands-on healing practices," I was deeply saddened by the release of the March U.S. Bishops' Guidelines for Evaluating Reiki as an Alternative Practice."
> The bishops' committee proclaimed that "since Reiki therapy is not compatible with either Christian teaching or scientific evidence, it would be inappropriate for Catholic institutions... or persons representing the Church...to promote or to provide support for Reiki therapy."

> It saddened me to see that a healing practice that has been widely embraced and shared through Catholic retreat and spirituality centers by lay and religious alike will now be effectively burned at the stake.
>
> Being neither theologian nor scientist, I cannot begin to argue the doctrinal perspectives of the bishops involved. Nor can I challenge the scientific studies that were consulted in issuing their statement. However, as a woman of faith, I need neither theologian nor scientist to decide for me if Reiki is, or is not, of God, or whether it is, or is not, an effective tool for healing.

Schmidt is not alone in her beliefs. Like many practitioners and recipients, she has fallen victim to one of Reiki's greatest dangers—deception, where she actually believes that she is being used by God. Perhaps she would be convinced otherwise, if she had had the experience of another Catholic seeker, Carol, who embraced Reiki after a "Protestant Reiki Master" volunteered to do a session to address the chronic back pain of Carol's spouse. She recalled:

> The first question I asked her was if this was something appropriate for Christians. The woman explained that Reiki had brought her much closer to God and enriched her faith. She said it was the same healing Jesus' disciples were able to do, and that the Holy Spirit is the entity who performs the healing. Describing the Holy Spirit as an intelligent, loving, universal healing energy, she said it always knows just what the patient needs, whether it is physical, emotional or spiritual healing. The frequency of the energy self-adjusts throughout the session in a way that the practitioner has no control over it. The energy could feel like heat radiating out of the palms, feel like a pulsing electrical sensation, or feel like nothing at all even if the patient could feel it powerfully. When we asked if the energy could possibly come from occult sources, she smiled and asked us why on earth Satan would ever want to help or heal someone. She passed on testimonials/

> stories from other Christians who experienced powerful conversion from their involvement in Reiki.
>
> I began to read books on Buddhism that suggested Christianity and Buddhism and have more in common than not in practical application. I became more interested in psychic phenomenon and my Reiki master explained that Reiki could keep you safe during astral projection, meditation, and even while visiting metaphysical fairs.... Alarm bells were going off, but I kept reasoning them away. (St. Padre Pio Center for Deliverance Counseling; SPCDC Spiritual Warfare BBS)

Eventually she was lead to a priest who informed her that Reiki had occult moorings. She renounced Reiki but was left with a stinging sensation in her hands, and she would occasionally feel the sensation of heat going up and down her spine. She has been led to accept that once a person is initiated into Reiki, it never goes totally away. She commented that she felt "...as though an angry entity were 'punishing' me for daring to cross it." Her husband still suffers from chronic back pain, but he has now embraced Catholicism. Having now experienced Reiki over time and having been exposed to its real dangers, her assessment of it is quite different, and her goal now is to warn everyone. In reflecting on her experiences, she stated:

> I urge all of you to warn everyone you know away from Reiki. It is pure evil disguised as something enticing and good. The mysterious "energy" comes from demonic entities that were channeled long ago by that Buddhist monk. (SPCDC Spiritual Warfare BBS)

What is sad about Carol's experience is that she is now relieved but not totally delivered. She is unaware of the fact that she can be set free from Reiki.

Reiki Dangers

The Harm: Spiritual

I vividly remember the responses of Reiki practitioners when I asked if Reiki could do any harm. In each instance, their answers reflected what was in most of the literature—a resounding "no." Prior to the start of my research, it would have been very difficult for me to comprehend how they could respond in that manner. They had ignored the wise counsel of the Bible; Jesus was rejected as God; the activities that practitioners engaged in—whether serving as a channel for "healing" energy or involvement with spirit-helpers—were clearly what the Bible called "detestable" practices. However, I now better understood the nature of their transformation because of their practice of Reiki. In the worldview that Reiki espoused, there is no real place for evil as it relates to the realm of the spirit. The logic is that everything is one and is connected to spirit. To speak of good or evil actually represents a duality that their worldview does not support. In fact, duality is an illusion born out of ignorance. Hence, if God as "spirit" is in everything and everything has God's spirit in it, there can be no real evil in any "spirit" because God is good. Moreover, if being a conduit of healing is good, the contact with spirits that helps or facilitates healing also has to be good. Such becomes the logic when the truth of the Bible becomes irrelevant.

Edward confirmed this faulty assumption when he talked about how, in his practice of Reiki, he grew increasingly suspicious of the counsel of the Bible. For a season, the truth of his experiences in Reiki held more significance than what he had known to be true in the Bible. One such perverted truth was his new perception of sin. He wrote, "*A big part of their teaching was that there is no evil, that 'sin' is a lie to bring fear and cause us to wander from our path. The step from doubting Jesus' mission was easy. Without the conviction of sin, salvation offered in Jesus' name made no sense. Damnation held no reality for me. With no ultimate penalty, who would have need of a Savior? This faulty reasoning all started with the premise that the Scripture lacked some greater truth, and all of Reiki is built to promote that belief"* (Harz, 32).

In rejecting the counsel of the Bible, the practitioners also choose to reject God. While each had a perception of self as being very "spiritual" with spirituality being defined loosely as "their sense of connection to God," perception of a connection and a lack of true relationship to a personal God had eternal consequences. They would not seek out that which they thought they had found. In so doing, unless God intervened, and in their view, God did not intervene or interfere, eventually they would stand before a Holy God having rejected the One sent to bring about authentic healing and restoration back to him. However, on that occasion of standing before him, while not a popular view, there would be no reincarnation or opportunity to circumvent the consequences of rejection. Paul's admonishment in his second letter to Timothy (2:12 AMP) concerning Jesus was absolute. "If we deny and disown and reject Him, He will deny and disown and reject us." Jesus was equally clear in Luke 10:16, "… He who rejects me rejects him who sent me." Therein is Reiki's greatest harm. It can void out any possible relationship with God through Jesus and cost practitioners their very souls.

In some ways, Edward's account of his journey into Reiki is reminiscent of the story of the Prodigal Son found in Luke 15:11-24 in that the son left the father, backslid, and came to his senses. The harm he ultimately experienced in going his own way caused him to return to his father. For Edward, the harm came in degrees. Driven by desire and lust, Edward strayed from the Father and admitted that he was willing to compromise anything, including his relationship to Jesus, as long as he could access the Reiki energy that he, through personal experience, identified as a demon. Although Edward found out later that true biblical Christianity was in conflict with his practice of Reiki, he recognized that practitioners didn't *"… want to close the door because once they bring you in, particularly once they take you into something like Reiki, once they open you to other demons, once you become demonized [under the influence of], the influence of that demon will wipe out the real power of your Christian faith. It'll take away your ability to make a difference as a Christian."* What Edward found out was that his ability to be a witness for Christ was virtually non-existent, *"... You can keep calling yourself a Christian 'til the day you die, but if [the spirit behind Reiki] has taken out your effectiveness, he doesn't care if we're all Christians. If we have no effectiveness, he has no worry."* However, Edward still felt he could be a witness, *"So even though I was practicing Reiki and telling people to seek Jesus, not a single one of them came to the Lord even when they were healed of terminal illnesses.... I had [healed] terminal people, but did it produce any good thing in their life? They're [just] still living."* Edward saw the harm of Reiki in his life on various levels. They were spiritual and relational. *"So it whittles away at the foundations of truth and the Gospel so that at some point either you have a meaningless Gospel and you have plenty of what you wanted or you're going to give up your other gods for the truth of the Gospel."* Edward realized that his faith and relationship to God was harmed.

This recognition compelled him to call into question the practitioners' insistence that "Reiki can do no harm" when he was given information about the symbols. *"When I went to get the Reiki two and one of the things they said was, 'You never leave this symbol written on a piece of paper that anybody could get a hold of it,' there was this imminent sense ...* [of harm] *for somebody to get a hold of it that wasn't ready for it. And the thing that goes through my mind at that point, 'Wait a minute, I thought Reiki wasn't supposed to be able to do anything that could harm anybody.' It was all good. If it's all good, what's the danger in letting somebody have it that's not ready? How could they not be ready if it's all good?"* While his mind was filled with many questions, he also was aware that there were activities he engaged in while he practiced Reiki that he would never have considered if he had not disregarded the counsel found in the Bible and broken his covenant relationship with God.

The Harm: Spiritual Bondage

One activity was the performance of the psychic surgery on one of his workers who had a torn kidney. Immediately following the Reiki session, his employee had some type of scope done that confirmed the infected area was now covered with scar tissue. Incredulously, I asked if physical "healing" actually took place in Reiki because most research only gave information about the perception of less pain and anxiety. Outside of a study done by Wetzel on hemoglobin and hematocrit levels, there was no hard empirical data on physical healing. However, there were many anecdotal stories. His response was very revealing. *"The demon can heal. It can physically create that change. What I've seen is it often comes with a bondage."* One of the bondages that Edward referenced was bondage or enslavement to occult activity. Already mentioned was his deep craving for this energy. Although married, Edward commented, *"I found myself ready to take off anywhere with this woman,* [the woman who had initiated him] *all to keep this new overwhelming energy."* This woman had experienced partial blindness in one eye and complete blindness in the other. Her sight had been restored through psychic surgery in the Philippines.

Beyond the psychic surgery and serving as a channel for frequent Reiki energy exchanges, he spoke of his openness to astral projection, telepathy, using spells, and clairvoyance. Moreover, he recalled the swallowing of ashes, known as vubuti, and drinking a fluid called the 'elixir of life'—both substances had been supernaturally produced out of nothing in the palm of a Hindu miracle worker many believed to be God. This was not only true in Edward's case but also true in the case of each practitioner I interviewed. However, I noticed that beyond having an openness to certain practices, they were actively involved in them. There was occasional to frequent activity with spirit guides, tarot cards, power animals, astrology, and channeled writing. Experiencing liminal or altered states of consciousness was a regular occurrence for most of the practitioners (Engebretson and Wardell, 2002). All regularly dealt with alleged psychic anatomies such as auras, meridians, chakras, and astral bodies (Mansour et al. 1999). Some admitted to practicing aspects of Buddhism and Hinduism. In talking about these activities, none showed any hint of defensiveness or guilt about these practices. With a transformed worldview, these practices were accepted and celebrated. Bearheart said it quite well when recalling her experience with her power animal while practicing Reiki, *"It's not for everybody, but it is something that is absolutely real in my world because I've seen too many instances."*

Outside of the very clear biblical warnings that were ignored, there have been researchers who have documented the side effects of trafficking in the occult. One such expert is Kurt Koch, a noted German theologian, minister, and evangelist, who for forty years counseled and ministered to many who struggled with occult bondage. He authored several critical works that addressed the topic of occult counseling. In *Christian Counseling and Occultism* (1994, 188), he listed the following psychological disturbances as side effects of occult subjugation or bondage:

1. Warping and distortion of character: hard, egoistic persons; uncongenial, dark natures

2. Extreme passions: abnormal sexuality; violent temper; belligerence; tendencies to addiction

3. Emotional disturbances: compulsive thoughts; melancholia; suicidal thoughts, anxiety states

4. Possession: destructive urges, fits of mania; tendency to violent acts and crime; inhabitation by [spirits]

5. Mental illness

6. Bigoted attitude against Christ and God: conscious atheism; simulated piety; indifference to God's Word and to prayer; blasphemous thoughts; religious delusions

7. Puzzling phenomena in their environment

This list in no way suggested what would definitely happen to everyone involved in Reiki. It simply demonstrated what has happened over time when individuals were opened up to spiritistic activities. What was observed clearly in each Reiki practitioner was a somewhat bigoted attitude towards Jesus, an indifference to God's Word, and frequent displays of puzzling phenomena in their environment. While I recognized that indifference towards God often had nothing to do with involvement in occult activities, that indifference coupled with involvement and acceptance of the practices mentioned could not be ignored. Pastor Norris, who not only counseled Edward but saw the harmful effects of Reiki on the wives of pastors in Suriname, observed:

> Well, harm is measured in layers or in degree. Uh, if all we're looking at is the benefit of someone's body being physically touched and, uh, "Did the pain in their arm go away or did their stomach ache disappear?" If that's the only way we measured validity, fine! If that was the only criteria of value, well then, fine! But there are other ways in which you can be harmed. You can be harmed spiritually; you can be harmed intellectually; you can be harmed relationally and what happens with Reiki is that it may, on the surface of it, at a very thin veneer, offer the prospect of doing some good. Yeah, sure, "Somebody's belly ache went away, isn't that wonderful. Okay? Praise the Lord." But at the deeper level, at other levels, at the intellectual, the biblical, the relational levels, uh, there's definitely harm being done. As Edward will point out, there's harm to your relationship with Jesus. Uh, there's a need that you're going to ultimately have to confront. Here's what Reiki teaches versus on the other hand, here's what the Bible teaches. Now you have to find a way to either harmonize that or something. One of those two things has to go.

The Harm: Psycho-Spiritual
Beyond the spiritual harm, there is the possibility creating the

conditions for a type of psycho-spiritual harm that often has a combination of physical, emotional and spiritistic manifestations. In some literature, the manifestations have been called Kundalini Reiki; in Hindu culture, *Shaktipat* or *Shitipat Disha*; and in western occult tradition, Kundalini Awakening or Arousal. It appeares that the Hindu explanation predates other definitions, so that is the definition that has been used to describe the experience. Swami Shivom Tirth (1997) in *A Guide to Shaktipat* commented:

> Shaktipat is the descent of...dormant spiritual energy... at the base of the spine.... Shaktipat, thus, means the descent of Chit-Shakti (the power of mind-stuff) of the Guru on the [mind stuff] of the disciple.... The awakening of Shakti has been described by all spiritual practices and theories with little difference but name.... The principle idea is that whatever system one follows, the end result is the awakening [transformation] of the inner-consciousness." (1–2)

In many cases, this transmittal of energy is mediated through the laying-on of hands. Sometimes, the energy is manifested because of participation in practices designed to alter or transform the consciousness.

The danger of awakening this force through dabbling with energy like Reiki was reinforced by occultist C.W. Leadbeater. In quoting directly from Leadbeater's book, *The Chakras*, Ashworth wrote "The force is a tremendous reality ... it is not a thing with which to play...for to experiment with it without understanding it is far more dangerous than it would be for a child to play with nitro-glycerin.... It brings liberation to Yogis and bondages to fools ..." (37). The reality was that it brought bondage to all. However, in the yogic tradition, the guru or yogi spent years having this energy integrated into his or her system. In Reiki, the energy was often transmitted into a person's system over a weekend session. Leadbeater would most likely consider a weekend initiation conditions for "premature arousal." Leadbeater noted that this arousal caused the energy to rush into the body instead of a flowing upwards and out. The effects were that the energy "... excites the most undesirable passions, excites and intensifies their effects to such a degree that it becomes impossible for the [person] to resist them because a force had been brought into play in whose presence [the individual] is as helpless as a swimmer before the jaws of shark" (Ashworth, 36). This was further supported in the monograph of Reiki Master David Ashworth and the article of Whisitt warning about the dangers of Reiki. O'Mathuna also warned about the dangers of dabbling with "life energies." Unlike Ashworth, who believed that the energy could be controlled, the distinction that both O'Mathuna and Whisitt made was that the energy should be avoided at all costs by everyone.

The Harm: Manifestations

Before leaving this discussion, it is critical again to point out that Reiki does not affect everyone in the same manner, especially in the beginning. However, based on the experience of Edward and support in the literature, there are some clear parallels between the experience of Reiki and the experience of the Kundalini Awakening.

Edward wrote about an incredible energy that went *"both up and down my body, covering me to the top of my head to the tips of my finger and to the tips of my toes. It was seductive beyond sexual … . I continued to feel that energy flow for more than a month"* (Harz, 4-5). In a follow-up discussion, he confirmed that some of the symptoms of Kundalini Awakening mirrored his experience of Reiki: *"Kundalini is a variation of Reiki."* Beyond his own experience, he recalled sending Susie Reiki at a distance: *"Now I understand what I sent to Susie as I saw it happening and she experienced it in Germany. I sent it and she received this experience while connected by phone—both of us in a meditative state. After my sending and her experiencing this opening of energy that flowed up her spine and burst out the top of her head, she described it to me exactly as I had seen it. Now I see that was in detail, the same description that these people call Kundalini Awakening or Kundalini Reiki. I never*

The Myth of Reiki Safety 169

knew anyone else had experienced it." El Collie (1995, n. p.) gave a list of Kundalini Awakening signs and symptoms. They included:

1) muscle twitches, cramps, or spasms, 2) energy rushes or immense electricity circulating the body, 3) involuntary bodily movements or feeling an inner force pushing one into postures or moving one's body in unusual ways, 4) burning heat or ice-cold currents moving up the spine, and in most cases reaching the head, 5) intensified or diminished sexual desires, 6) numbness, 7) mental confusion or difficulty focusing, 8) fast pulse and increased metabolism, 9) hearing inner sound or sounds; 10) altered states of consciousness sometimes accompanied by heightened awareness, spontaneous trance states, mystical experiences; 11) heat, strange activity, and/or blissful sensations in the head, particularly in the crown area, 12) psychic experiences such as E.S.P., out-of-body experiences, past-life memories, astral travel, awareness of auras, chakras, contact with spirit guides through inner voices, visions, healing power, 13) ecstasy, bliss and intervals of tremendous joy, love, peace, and compassion, 14) intensified understanding and sensitivity, insight into one own essence, deeper understanding of spiritual truths 15) enlightenment experiences consisting of direct knowing of a more expansive reality or transcendent awareness.

Similar symptoms have been supported by Greenwall (1988), Grof and Grof (1989) and Romain (1991) who sought to merge his experience of Kundalini Awakening with Christian spirituality, although he offered that the experience took place for him as he fell into a semi-trance state, frequently referred to as an altered state of consciousness. Parallels have often been drawn to the aspects of Kundalini Awakening and Christ-based Spirit baptism. However, as stressed by Ankerberg and Weldon (1996), "According to the Bible ... receiving the Holy Spirit is not about having occult experiences" (609). Again, the litmus test of the experience is whether it has support in Scripture and direction towards or away from the biblical Christ.

Outside of Edward's and the other practitioners' experiences of Reiki and even the descriptions of Kundalini Awakening, what validated the likely connection between the two experiences were the documented accounts of the Reiki experience found in Engebreston and Wardell's (2002) descriptive study involving twenty-three participants. In reflecting on the 30-minute sessions, they reported the following findings based on participant responses. They offered:

> Participants reported numbness, involuntary muscle twitching, and feelings of heat, which clustered into sensations in temperature, sound,… and discordant sense of touch…. Another stated, "I tried to sense my pulse (as I did in Transcendental Meditation), and I couldn't find my heartbeat after a while doing this.…" Sensations of temperature included internal and external feelings of "warmth" and "a centered glow."… Some felt cold and warm simultaneously.… One participant commented on the "soft soothing music, (I) liked the music," but no music was playing.…
> Participants described feelings in their bodies they equated with "energy." Descriptors included "pulsing," "throbbing," "strobe," "surge," "electricity," and "sensation of a current" … like a charge … all the way to my toes…. Some reported sensations of feeling the Reiki Master's hands in areas where they were not physically present or in several places at the same time…. Most participants reported feeling relaxed…. Some reported feelings of "nervousness," "a built up energy.…" Cognitive or mental experiences included feelings of detachment and clarity…. Other responses included being "unable to focus," and "addlebrained." (52)

While reporting some physiological changes in blood pressure and other factors that indicated relaxation, it was concluded that "liminal [or altered] states of consciousness are reported as optimal states for healing" (Ward, 1989). It was recognized that altered states of consciousness could be precipitated by activity not related to the occult (i.e., daydreams and sleep). However, "Almost any continually cultivated altered state is at least, potentially capable of producing spirit encounters" (Ankerberg and Weldon, 21). Tal Brooks, in *Riders of the Cosmic Circuit,* noted that altered states were one of the vehicles essential for interaction with spirits and possession. Ankerberg and Weldon (1993) and Warwick Montgomery (1976) saw altered states as having the ability to "open a person to the supernatural realm and contact with spirits who are really demons" (Ankerberg and Weldon, 23). The often bizarre manifestation of many of these symptoms led many to seek out the help of those who were involved in transpersonal counseling. Transpersonal counseling specifically dealt with individuals whose experience "involving entities and realms that are not objectively real according to a Western worldview" indicated a "Spiritual Emergency" (Grof and Grof 1989, 12). The transpersonal counselors often had personal experience with or were knowledgeable of similar experiences.

The Harm: Spiritual Emergencies

The term, popularized by Stanislav and Christina Grof (1989), editors of *Spiritual Emergency: When Personal Transformation Becomes a Crisis,* was used to explain away the harm encountered in occult experiences. They recognized that these experiences were very dangerous but suggested they had the potential for healing. They reasoned, "If properly understood and treated as difficult stages in a natural developmental process, spiritual emergencies can result in spontaneous healing of various emotional and psychosomatic disorders, favorable personality changes ... and evolution toward what some call 'higher consciousness'" (7). Weldon and Ankerberg (1996) defined a spiritual emergency as a "reinterpretation of the pathological phenomena induced by occult practice—as a positive transforming spirituality ('a spiritual emergence')" (598). They gave further insight as to the harmful effects this "reinterpretation" had on a particular occult experience. They observed: "In the case of Kundalini...[awakening] symptoms of mental illness and demonization are gratuitously redefined as emerging manifestations of "higher" or divine consciousness. Thus, we are not to question or fear the Kundalini process but to surrender to it and trust it implicitly, for it is indeed part of that ageless wisdom of evolutionary transformation, which is far wiser than ourselves" (598). This was true in Edward's initial experience and again, as in the practice of Reiki, the notion of "surrendering" to a process resurfaced.

The Grofs gave a list of the types of "spiritual emergencies" for which they provided counseling. The list included: "the shamanic crisis, the awakening of the Kundalini...the crisis of psychic opening (i.e., ESP, clairvoyance), past-life experiences, communications with spirit guides and 'channeling,'..., and possession states" (13–14).

To facilitate the handling of the many challenges individuals were experiencing, call centers were situated around the country under the umbrella of the Spiritual Emergence Network (S.E.N.) Distressed callers were directed to a counselor who shared a similar belief system and validated their experience. The counselor attempted to refer them to three potential helpers in their geographic location who volunteered to assist them in their psycho-spiritual crisis. The major problem of S.E.N. and other such "transpersonal" counseling centers was that people who sought them out were like drug addicts who were sent to drug houses for support from other addicts; there was no real relief because the counsel given usually led to deeper bondage. The advice given "not only help[s] undergird and legitimize the occult, but it effectively inhibits discernment of the true issues involved" (Ankerberg and Weldon, 1996, 598).

When a person comes under spiritual attack because he or she has dabbled with the occult, rather than see the anguish and torture as a warning from God that the practice is immoral and spiritually dangerous, the person is deluded into believing that the pain is part of the process. Hence, the practice is legitimized, the ability to discern the spiritual and dangerous nature of the problem is explained away, and the person remains in occult bondage. Edward experienced a similar explaining away of the truth when he first encountered the unnatural changes that affected his body upon his initiation into Reiki.

The conclusion drawn is that outside of the obvious harm that Reiki has on a participant's relationship to God, even if it went undetected, Edward's experiences and the literature confirm a very real threat. Any practice that is designed to open a person up to other spiritual realities or transform the consciousness of an individual is fraught with eventual harm. Although the Grofs did not mention Reiki by name, Reiki's similarity to the Kundalini Awakening cannot be denied. The reality that transpersonal counseling and S.E.N. exist validates the fact that eventually occult activities lead to a spiritual crisis. While the activities are not articulated as "occult activities," reinterpreting the experience through transpersonal counseling to be more reflective of a worldview that is not grounded in biblical theism does not serve to eradicate the harmful effects.

Under scrutiny, the claims that Reiki can do no harm have not been sustained in the literature or in the experience of Edward. His involvement drew him away from God and put his relationship to Jesus in serious jeopardy. Moreover, for the Reiki practitioners, at risk are their eternal souls even if they cannot discern that reality.

The Harm: Two Different Realities

In looking at the level of occult bondage that practitioners embraced and the eventual consequences, not much discernment was needed to confirm that there were two distinct spiritual realities at work. One spiritual reality was an impersonal unknowable energy that did not differentiate between good and evil but supported a worldview that was antagonistic towards biblical Christianity and God. Attempts to characterize this energy as natural and non-invasive proved unconvincing. This energy seemed to possess a highly intelligent mind of its own and desired surrender from its recipients. Note the paradox in practitioners' description. Reiki is impersonal, yet it thinks independently. Moreover, regardless of the name, this energy seemed essential to the practice of occult activities. Strangely enough, accessing Reiki energy gave insight and counsel to practitioners. I have called "perceived" benefits of this practice, the fruit of Reiki.

The Fruit of Reiki

Ephesians 6:10-13 (KJV) serves as a reminder "that we wrestle not against flesh and blood but against powers, principalities, rulers of darkness, and spiritual wickedness in high places." The implication is that while certain behaviors and practices have been advanced through human agents, there is a spiritual force behind the scenes motivating the action. The Bible clearly warns in Matthew 7:16 (NIV), "By their fruit, you will recognize them." Beyond reading journals and books about Reiki, I had the experience of observing practitioners over time. It was from observing them over time, allowing them to tell their personal stories, and actually interviewing them that I was able to draw conclusions about their spiritual journey and how it ultimately produced what I've called the "fruit" of Reiki. In interviewing practitioners, I discovered that:

1. Family background, especially the relationship to the father or the authority figure, played a pivotal role in influencing spiritual path.

2. Personal crisis resulted in spiritual hunger, but the void was not filled by a relationship with Jesus.

3. Early supernatural experiences seemed to direct away from the God of the Bible but opened individuals up to various spiritual/supernatural experiences.

4. Family backgrounds with "occult" activity seemed to affect the next generation.

5. All came from family backgrounds that espoused Judeo-

Christian moorings. Each practitioner at some point rejected some aspect of the presentation of God in their respective denominations.

6. While the notion of salvation may have been a factor at some point, most did not presently claim a personal relationship with God through accepting Jesus although each saw themselves as very spiritual.

7. The spiritual path seemed to confirm an initial theistic worldview that later became mixed with a decidedly pantheistic worldview, also know as syncretism, replete with "many paths to God."

8. Generally, there was a belief in reincarnation and a general neutrality expressed towards the spirit realm. Evil and a "real" devil were dismissed.

9. The Spiritual Experience/Interest Inventory (a survey that I administered to assess occult activities) indicated a high level of involvement and interest in spiritual practices that, for the most part, would be called "occult" or anti-biblical spiritual activity.

10. While the term "Trinity" was intellectually assented to by some, the depiction of the individual members of the Trinity was usually distinct from what is represented in the Bible. Specific questions about the Godhead were met with some level of defensiveness and surprise as to their relationship to healing.

11. God as Father was seen as "he" or "she." He was the Creator who was loving, kind, and merciful. He "minded his business" and did not judge, demand, or interfere.

12. Jesus was an extraordinary person who reflected one of the paths to God, but he was not God in the biblical sense. Because man is "innately divine," Jesus was God as much as every other human was God. He was more evolved, but he was not sinless.

13. The counsel of the Bible was generally rejected and not perceived as an inerrant and authoritative guide. Objective truth did not exist. Truth was based on one's perception—very much in keeping with postmodernism.

14. In addressing the Holy Spirit, there was an intellectual assent that he was the performer of miracles; however, he was generally independent of working in concert with the rest of the Godhead, especially Jesus. The Holy Spirit was a force.

15. Reiki seemed to represent a spirit that was perceived as holy and another name for God. This god was intelligent impersonal energy that animated from all things, human and non-human.

16. Reiki healing emanated from the Universal Mind or Consciousness. Reiki brought a healing presence and allowed individuals to be open to their innate healing abilities.

17. Reiki healing gave insight and spirit counsel; emphasis was placed on surrendering and constantly performing Reiki on self and others.

18. Reiki healing ability normally stemmed from initiations, secret ceremonies and symbols, mantras and attunements. However, it was possible to receive Reiki through a massage like Edward did.

19. Reiki healing was tied to sound and vibration levels. An attempt was made to connect Reiki to quantum physics.

20. Physical healings included accelerated wound healing, lowering of blood count, alleviation of headaches, and disappearance of cervical cancer.

21. Practitioners generally became Reiki evangelists who believed that many paths lead to God, and each path is valid.

22. Practitioners served as channels who worked with invisible auras, meridians, and chakras. They noted that all spirits of light should be accepted.

23. The notion of the Cross, the suffering of Jesus, and repentance as criteria for spiritual healing was rejected.

24. The experience of Reiki was accompanied by various psychic phenomena. The hands of the practitioner usually became very hot or cold as the energy flowed.

25. Often healing was facilitated by spirit guides, psychic surgery, and power animals connected to Shamanism.

26. While lip service was paid to Christianity, many biblical truths were rejected. However, the concepts of Taoism, Buddhism, Hinduism, and Shamanism were strongly supported.

27. Reiki healing opened up practitioners to a variety of spiritual practices that would be considered "occult activities" by biblical standards.

28. With the practice of Reiki came a variety of "latent" abilities such as clairvoyance, clairaudience, and healing.

29. Generally, individuals felt transformed by Reiki and seemed almost addicted to the energy from Reiki.

30. The greater the involvement in Reiki, the greater the rejection of the Bible and biblical Christianity as both narrow and judgmental.

31. There was a strong sense that Reiki was from God and that practitioners would eventually return to God. However, Reiki healing pointed away from Jesus. This return to God did not include judgment but did embrace reincarnation and Karma.

32. While the consensus was that Reiki could do no harm, one practitioner spoke at length about the great spiritual harm caused by Reiki and called Reiki a demon. The description given of the initial transmission of Reiki energy mirrored a very dangerous Hindu practice known as "Kundalini Rising."

33. The criterion for measuring the efficacy of Reiki healing was that "it works." However, the results were not consistent. Reiki energy went to where it was needed, undirected by the practitioner.

34. While submitting that Reiki works, one practitioner confirmed that Reiki healing was generally accompanied by some type of bondage.

35. It was possible for a compromised Christian to come under the influence of Reiki. Without discernment, it was also possible to be deceived into believing that, on the surface, Reiki is biblical and all healing is from God.

36. The only way to be free of Reiki and its influence was repentance, salvation, acceptance of the counsel found in the Bible, the intercession of a spiritually mature Christian, and the work of the Holy Spirit as passionately talked about by Edward, a former practitioner.

The Myth of Reiki Safety 179

The obvious question is what manner of spirit or energy would wield this level of influence? Ankerberg and Weldon (1991) offered, "We believe that the energy that does exist is spiritism or spiritically used energy; that is, various natural energies either used by spirits in the energy manifestations or the spirits themselves falsely interpreted as the working of 'completely natural', 'human' or 'divine' energies" (68–69). When Ankerberg and Weldon arrived at their initial conclusions about energy, they also acknowledged that the characteristics that they had discovered to be true about "energy" were also true of demonic spirits. Former Reiki practitioner Edward made the same assessment. While it is easy for someone to be dismissive about an unproven theory or hypothesis about Reiki, it is much more difficult to dismiss the actual experience of a former practitioner and the striking similarity it has to related practices. Not only does being involved in Reiki produce a verbal fruit that alters how God is perceived, it also produces fruit which manifests in what many would call occult activity. One thing that stood out to me as I interviewed Edward was his comment, "Reiki opens you up." One practice he embraced was psychic surgery. While I have already mentioned the experience, his actual experience in his own words bears repeating. He recalled:

> As with my Reiki initiation, my psychic surgery experience was not brought on by form or ceremony, but instead it came as I remained open to any spirit that would come to/or through me. Any Reiki session: private meditation, treating someone, or group sharing all started with opening our spiritual being. At times I even saw the demons, in the spirit realm, as beings of light in their various colors.
>
> Merv was an employee who told me he was passing blood. He had had a tear in his kidney before and was sure the same had happened again. I offered him Reiki but he had an appointment with his doctor. When the doctor, for reasons not given, postponed the appointment, Merv decided to try the

Reiki. That same day he showed me in the toilet bowl that his urine had turned pink from the blood.

That night Merv came over to my home. He laid on the floor of my living room with me sitting alongside him. After the usual clearing my mind and opening myself to what would come, I put my hands over him. My usual experience of healing was by feeling the subtle lack of heat in an area of the body and replacing that with the energy that flowed from my hands. But as I moved my hands down the chakra positions, I could see down inside his body. In his spirit there was a black mass. (Its location, he told me later, was the area of his pain.) With one hand I found I could draw the mass by raising my hand while in the spirit realm remaining connected to it. I drew it up and out of his body and continued his treatment in the usual form. The pain was gone immediately and the physical healing was confirmed.

Although he called himself Christian as I did at the time, his life showed no sign of an inner change. In the following months and years his integrity grew worse. One of the most telling signs to me was that I could sometimes heal their body, but their lives grew worse instead of improving. I never saw someone who was healed with Reiki that really praised Jesus or progressed in their walk with the Lord.

Susie, who I always contacted concerning my experiences, later told me that I should have made sure to remove that black mass from my home. It was unhealthy and dangerous to leave in it my house. I never saw it again nor experienced a harmful effect from that darkness, but such are the fears and sometime real dangers of dealing in demonic things with demonic devices.

Bearheart, a Reiki practitioner who I had visited and interviewed, identified with being a shaman. She gave an example of how Reiki and Shamanism served to emotionally help a man who was grieving the loss of a child. *"I didn't really think about Shamanism* and Reiki in one breath until one day I was working on a man who had had some really heart-breaking circumstances. *A babysitter killed his child. Put it in the oven and baked it. I mean just the most unspeakable, horrible, worse than the worst movie you could imagine. And so he—to keep himself, I think, from being totally destroyed—he worked four jobs and slept not a lot."* This man was a psychologist who asked that this session be done because he was trying to have Reiki offered at the site he worked at and reasoned it would be easier to present if he had the experience.

> *So, working on him and getting—he zonked out—full of questions, very left brain and that's why I gave him the breathing exercise to do to get him quiet and allow him to relax. When you do breath work, your body relaxes, your blood pressure comes down, your brain wave pattern shifts, you go into an altered state [of consciousness], the body's happy, brain makes happy chemicals, it may have a slight analgesic affect so you may even help a headache or something, just cool out. And I'm working along, all the positions on the head, on the shoulders and in the upper chest and then I get to the heart and you start often breathing with your client, especially when you really establish rapport....*
>
> *[Well] I could feel somebody standing next to me. Now I know that no one came through that door but I could feel somebody standing there. So I thought, "I know this is no one physical, but I can't resist looking," and of course I couldn't see anybody. And so I went by and I called out mentally, "Who's here" to my power animal. [I asked, "Out of Shamanism?"] Yeah. Uh, everyone has one at birth whether or not they're aware of it.... They give you strength—they give you also increased strength and lack of susceptibility to illness and so on. Here's this great big power animal—...my primary power animal is a black bear—this was a silver tip grizzly, huge, extremely powerful ...and I had already started in with the level two to talk to the [the man's] heart and try and provide some level of comfort.*

> And when you are at that point, you've...used the symbols and the mantras to open that line of communication....
> And so I'm sort of mentally saying to the grizzly, "I can't talk to you now, I'm working." And he [the bear] said to me, "I'm not here for you; I'm here for him." I went, "Oh, okay." It's like the surgeon standing back and saying, "Okay, you can go in there."...There are a variety of helpers that have a specifically strong healing wisdom and bear is one of them. And he worked on the heart and then stood back and said to me, 'Okay, he's yours.' I finished the session; [the psychologist] had a wonderful time. He expressed the feeling that his chest and heart felt more open, and I was saying nothing because I thought, "This will just freak him right out."
> It's not for everybody, but it is something that is absolutely real in my world because I've seen too many instances. And later on in reflecting about this because you keep notes of every session that you do if you have respect for your clients, I thought, "Why—I mean this is"—I was doing Reiki, "Why is this?" And then I thought about it. When you call out to the world of spirit, you call out to the great mystery, "Please put the power here," which is translation for the first symbol. As you know, the Buddha in me greets the Buddha in you, or my mind speaks to your mind. Any of the things that you are in effect saying to draw in a particular influence so that you can have that conversation. You are in conversation with what some people would call the spirit world.

One might think that Bearheart's stories about her involvement in Reiki were anomalies, but they were not. Venus, another Reiki practitioner interviewed, told me about spirit guides that assisted her and gave her insight and images when she performed Reiki. Venus offered, *"You know so much depends on the person's intention when they get on the table...."*

Shamanism, psychic surgery, and contact with spirit guides are not practices that find any support in biblical Christianity. The spirit behind Reiki is ultimately a spirit against Christ. The enemy, who is the father of lies, would like nothing better than to snare people with something that looks and feels God-like—healing. Already, he has done a credible job of convincing practitioners that he does not really exist. In 2 Corinthians 11:14, he often "masquerades as an angel of light." However, if one critically examines the facts surrounding the "energy" of Reiki and its subsequent fruit, it is self-evident that the intent of the practice is to ultimately draw people away from the true God and not towards Him.

The long-term effect of dabbling with the "energy" of Reiki is occult bondage. Although the process happens gradually for some, the spirits that are behind Reiki eventually reveal themselves in word and deed. Based on conversations with Edward, spiritual forces described as "energy" do not mind that recipients feel they are in control. The perception of control only lasts for a season. The words of Miles and Rand ring true. Reiki is not a force one masters; the force eventually masters those using the energy. Healing is not the final goal. The goal is to snare the soul and bind the will so that the practitioners or recipients involved would be unable to respond to the call of Jesus. Despite the horrific implications, there is a remedy. While the enemy is able to mimic healing to snare souls, the role of Christ as Savior and healer of the spirit cannot be replicated. Furthermore, the distinct role of the Holy Spirit who works in concert with Jesus cannot be duplicated.

The Reality of Biblical Healing 16

The Work of the Spirit in Healing

The Work of the Holy Spirit in Spiritual Healing

It would be impossible to talk about the fruit of Christ-based healing if there was no conversation about the Spirit behind Christ-based healing. There are two distinct spiritual realities at work in the discussion on biblical healing. The spiritual forces supporting the practice of Reiki are against Christ and ultimately against the people who have been snared by the practice of it. When practitioners reference this spirit, they simply refer to it as "spirit." However, the Spirit at work in Christ-based healing is the Holy Spirit. He is the third person of the Godhead, and he testifies of Jesus according to John 15:26.

In the initial conversations with those who had experienced Christ-based healing, the Holy Spirit was at work as the Paraclete or Counselor even prior to their physical experience of healings. Recipients of Christ-based physical healing came to acknowledge that prior to salvation, they had a major problem. They were spiritually sick because the power of sin dominated their lives. They did not arrive at that conclusion on their own; the Holy Spirit convicted them of sin and drew them to Jesus. Once each of them agreed with God's Word concerning their hopeless state and responded affirmatively to the redemptive plan of Jesus, it was the Holy Spirit who regenerated their lives by coming to dwell inside each of them. The initial hope offered by the Holy Spirit as He directed them to the Word of God was that they were saved—rescued. They would not have to pay the debt that had been incurred through sin. It had been cancelled, and they would now spend eternity with God, instead of experiencing his wrath. Jesus aptly told his disciples in Luke 10:20 (NIV), "… Rejoice that your names are written in heaven."

On this new journey with God, additional hope is offered through the Word when Jesus promised his disciples that the Holy Spirit mentioned in John 14:16-17 would be with all believers forever and guide them into all truth (John 16:13). Pastor Alexis recalled how the Holy Spirit told her the truth about why her physical healing would not manifest. She was full of anxiety and not faith. The Holy Spirit sanctified each participant of Christ-based healing and helped each to do things that pleased God. Mabel remembered how the Holy Spirit taught her and "[made] the desires of Jesus clear." For each of them, the Holy Spirit helped them to believe God's Word about spiritual healing found in Romans 10:13 and to stand in faith. The Holy Spirit empowered each to become witnesses for Christ and lead others to him. Acts 1:8 (NIV) confirmed this truth, "But you will receive power when the Holy Spirit comes on you, and you will be my witnesses."

The Work of the Holy Spirit in Physical Healing

When each of the recipients received Christ-based physical healing, the work of the Holy Spirit was manifested. Mark 16:18 (NIV) proclaims, "You shall lay hands on the sick and they shall recover." The Holy Spirit empowered Pastor Norris to lay hands on the crippled woman in Suriname, and she was healed immediately. Pastor Norris and a number of pastors anointed his wife with oil and laid hands on her paralyzed body while she lay bed-ridden in intensive care. When she recovered, each recognized that the power for healing was from the Holy Spirit. Even in anointing with oil, a practice found in James 5:14 regarding the sick, it is recognized that biblical use of oil is symbolic of the presence of the Holy Spirit. However, there is no power in the oil. In instances where simply the recitation of the Word of God and prayer and healing occurred, the Holy Spirit was at work. Finally, the Holy Spirit allowed countless souls to receive Christ when the Word of God preceded the miraculous. So in each life, the Holy Spirit was working "behind the scenes," informally providing instruction and counsel. Each instance of healing by God's Holy Spirit reflected or pointed back to Jesus.

The Sovereignty of the Holy Spirit in Healing

Before leaving this topic of the Holy Spirit at work, it must be noted that in Christ-based healing, conditions must be met, another distinction between the spirits behind Reiki healing and the Holy Spirit. While Reiki healing represents healing energy that can be accessed at anytime, the issue of God's sovereignty is generally overlooked. While practitioners talked and the literature confirmed the notion of surrendering to Reiki and allowing the energy to go wherever it was needed, there was rarely any conversation to indicate whether healing in this manner was the will of God. Bearheart spoke at one point how early in her practice of Reiki, before sending it to a friend diagnosed with cancer, she prayed. *"I ran upstairs and put my hands on a pillow and talked to God and said, 'You know, I don't know what you're going to do and you'll do whatever is appropriate. My preference, for whatever that may count, is that she live to be an old person and healthy.'"* Moreover, she then proceeded to send Reiki to her friend. However, the "how" of Reiki is not a method that can find support in the Bible. Regardless of apparent results, healing practices which violate God's sovereign way of doing things as dictated by the Bible certainly are not how the Holy Spirit works. The spirits behind Reiki work counter to the Holy Spirit's way of operating. The Holy Spirit always affirms and works in concert with the Word and will of God as Father.

Pastor Norris reflected on how a dear woman of God, very much like a mother figure to him, was very ill:

> She developed cancer and it took her two or three years to die. Especially in the last stages, I would visit her every day in the hospital; I would go and I would pray and I would pray that the Lord would touch her, that the Lord would heal her. And this one night I went in to pray for her and I'm ready to lay hands and pray—her husband's there, her doctor, who happened to be a good friend of mine, was there too and we were ready to lay hands and they all bowed their heads and I'm ready to pray for her healing and I heard the Lord say, "Not tonight!" And it was a shock when I heard that. "Not tonight!" So, I just prayed for the Lord's peace and I walked out of the place. Uh, ... twenty to thirty minutes later, she was dead.... Well, first of all, I was—I was in grief with her death, but I reflected on that a lot—a lot throughout that whole period of time, especially that night, the following days. And I was really re-encouraged and blessed by the fact that the Lord had said that. It showed me that her death wasn't an accident or happenstance or the Lord's failure; it was part of a plan.
>
> And suddenly—you know, that makes it okay for me. Uh, for me the bottom line is I want to stay at the center of God's will. I want to stay not one inch outside of that. If there's a healing that's in the center of God's will, I want to be there and I want to proclaim it and I want to watch the Lord do it. But if that healing is a millimeter outside of the center of God's will, I don't want to be involved in it. And that's where Reiki comes in. I want to be at the center of God's will and here is this lady whose death was at the center of God's will. And He told me that when He said, 'Not tonight'. It was his way of saying, 'Okay, I'll take it from here.... I'm taking her home; you've done your thing but now let me be Lord.' And it was—it's so sweet to hear that.... Everything was exactly according to his will, according to his time—it was perfect.

Reiki practitioners admit that sometimes death represents healing. On the surface, that admission seems reflective of surrender to the sovereignty of "spirit." However, a distinction must again be made. The Holy Spirit told Pastor Norris not to pray for this woman any longer. He obeyed, recognizing that this woman was going home to be with God because she had come into relationship with God through Jesus many years ago. In another healing, an angry and bitter man lay dying in the hospital. He called for Pastor Norris:

> So I went dutifully and—to pray for him and found out that he was dying of cancer. And I said, 'Well, I'll pray for healing, but are you prepared to go to be with Jesus, and so forth?' And he started cursing me out, 'What the hell do you mean?'...'I don't want this kind of stuff, get out of here.' And he kicked me out of the room. Well, the next day, I get another phone call—same guy, 'Would you please come back, I'm sorry.' So I went back. And this time, he's really, really sick and really close to dying. And I said, 'You know, Bill, we can pray for healing, but are you prepared?' And he looked at me with honest eyes and said, 'What do you mean, what do you mean prepared, what do you mean ready?' So I explained what it means to be ready and as I'm explaining I knew he was listening because he just suddenly stops looking at me, sits up in bed, I don't know where he got the energy from—sits up in bed and he's looking at a wall, I thought it was the wall and he starts saying, 'Thank you for forgiving me; I forgive this person; I forgive that person; I'm sorry I've ever done this; I'm sorry I've ever done that.' He's talking, not to me, but when he's finished with his litany of, 'I'm sorry for this and I'm sorry for that,' he looks at me, still sitting up in bed, I'm sitting next to the bed, and says, 'Well, I'm ready.' Lies back down, within 10 seconds, he was dead.... That's healing.

The difference was that at death, Pastor Norris wanted to make sure that the man was spiritually healed. Therefore, again, the Holy Spirit of God was present at this man's deathbed, convicting him of his need for Jesus before he transitioned into eternity and stood before God. This man was given the wonderful opportunity to address his spiritual sickness. He was confronted with the Truth of the Bible. He was a sinner who needed to surrender his life to Christ. In a short period, the Holy Spirit allowed the dying man to be directed towards Jesus thereby transforming his life and eternal destiny.

The Fruit of Biblical Healing

Similar to the Reiki practitioners, I had the opportunity to observe, listen to the personal stories, and conduct interviews with four individuals who had been recipients of Christ-based healing. While each was able to give a miraculous account of God touching their physical bodies, the healing that each of them felt was most important was salvation—the healing of their spirits. Thus, in talking about the "fruit" of biblical healing, all healing, whether it was spiritual, physical, mental, or emotional seemed to point back to Christ and was in harmony with the triune Godhead. In talking with recipients of Christ-based healing, I discovered:

1. Participants came from family backgrounds that had Judeo-Christian moorings. While most spoke of having a "religious" background, most indicated there was no "relationship" with God.

2. Unusual supernatural experiences seemed to direct towards the God of the Bible.

3. Personal crisis often resulting from the consequences of wrong behavior precipitated the initial experience of salvation.

4. Responses to the Spiritual Experience/Interest Inventory indicated no interest or involvement in any of the occult practices mentioned.

5. Any family connection to any activity considered "occult" in nature was renounced and repented of prior to or at salvation.

6. All subscribed to a biblically theistic worldview that accepted a triune Godhead.

7. God was Father and Creator.

8. Being a Christian meant having a personal relationship with God through Jesus Christ. The exclusive and only path to God was through Jesus.

9. Jesus, while seen as Son, Savior, Lord, and Healer, was also recognized as God.

10. The Holy Spirit was also God. He was the third person of the Godhead who led and guided into truth. He was not an impersonal force but a person.

11. Healing was perceived on a variety of levels—spiritual, physical, emotional, and mental.

12. Healing of the spirit or salvation was viewed as the most important healing. Repentance, belief, and acceptance in Jesus were essential in healing of the spirit.

13. Healing was a work of God based on the finished work of Jesus through the power of the Holy Spirit.

14. Healing could and did take place without the laying-on of hands. Prayer and faith in God's Word were critical factors in healing.

15. Physical healings were often very dramatic and resulted in restoration of sight, crippled bodies mended, dissolution

of masses, and eradication of life-threatening diseases. Sometimes those laying-on hands talked of feeling the sensation of heat or tingling in their hands.

16. Healing sometimes meant that the individual being prayed for died and went to be with the Lord.

17. Salvation or healing of the spirit was transformative in nature and evoked lifestyles of sanctification and obedience to God.

18. Spirit baptism played a vital role in sanctification and operation in spiritual gifts.

19. Physical healing always led to greater devotion to God and lifestyles of service to the will of God.

20. Healing was connected to the Cross and the suffering of Jesus. All healing had to point to Jesus.

21. The objective standard to evaluate any healing was only to be found in the Bible.

22. Physical healing was based on God's sovereignty and the revelation of healing in His Word.

23. The Word of God was the standard for all truth and the final authority for decisions.

There was no harm associated with authentic Christ-based healing.

Setting Captives Free 17

In Luke 4:18, Jesus talked about how the Spirit of the Lord was upon him, and he was anointed to set captives free. Many have been snared by Reiki and have not recognized its bondage. They believe that Reiki is a gift from God. Hopefully, all that has been written and discussed about Reiki has convinced many of Reiki's inherent dangers. For those who have not been snared by Reiki, it would be easy to judge the actions of practitioners and recipients and wonder how they could be so deceived. The reality is that deception is likely if the truth of the Bible is not known or the truth is known but rejected. In a postmodern age where truth is believed to be very subjective and the Bible for many is no longer the objective standard by which actions are judged, Reiki, especially in its early stages can seem like light. Many have talked about feelings of peace and relaxation, sensations of heat, tingling, and warmth. Some have experienced dramatic physical, mental, or emotional changes. Many could argue that they have had similar experiences in a Pentecostal or Charismatic church but with far different results. What should now stand out as different is the source and purpose of the healing as well as the long term fruit. Are individuals closer or further away from the God of the Bible who declares that Jesus is God and heals by the power of the Holy Spirit? If the response is "no" to any part of the question, then the individual must be redeemed (rescued) since *Reiki cannot be redeemed.*

Ministering to Reiki Practitioners/Recipients.
In talking with a practitioner or recipient of Reiki, it is important to draw them with cords of God's love. That is really God's optimal way of bringing correction. In the process, the person must be made to feel that they are valued by God and you. To demoralize or demonize them will only serve to make them very defensive. Keep in mind that a spiritual battle is taking place, and that battle is best won through prayer. Ask God to permit an opportunity where you are able to have a conversation, not an argument. Ultimately, the practitioner/recipient must understand that any healing derived from Reiki is a counterfeit of genuine biblical healing. Often times, those involved will attempt to justify the practice by the seemingly "good" results. Again, those involved must be helped to understand that God would never sanction a practice that leads them to disobey his Word. The truth is that Reiki opens doors to other practices. For those who say that they are not pursuing any other "occult" activity, it is important to point out that even if they are espousing biblical Christianity, practicing Reiki will seriously compromise their relationship with Christ. If they are espousing a belief system other than Christianity, they must still be made aware of the fact that Reiki does not represent the type of healing done by Jesus of the Bible. Reiki is not a reinterpretation of biblical healing as some have argued.

Sincerely Wrong
One thing that often stands out about practitioners is their level of compassion for others and their sincerity. They really do believe that they have touched the heart of God when they serve as channels for Reiki. God is seen as loving and kind, someone who desires to alleviate pain and suffering. Thus, practitioners are nurtured by the notion that they are serving God by relieving the suffering of others. For those who do not talk about God in particular, but reference Universal Mind or Universal spirit, they too believe that they have tapped into something that is intrinsically good. For the recipient, if Reiki relieves any symptoms of pain or discomfort, what

is most important to them is that "Reiki works." If their perception remains unchanged, they inadvertently become Reiki evangelists. What they sell to others is the fact that it worked for them. Those ministering to them must also have the capacity to "hear their story." Dragging someone to the "altar" or calling out "spirits" most likely will not work. It is a process. The person involved must ultimately understand that Reiki is a counterfeit of biblical healing, and they must also want to be freed from it. Again, the only way that understanding will come for most is through prayer and those willing to exemplify the compassion of Christ.

Seeking God for the Truth About Reiki

In Jeremiah 29:13 (NIV), God speaks, "You will seek me and find me when you seek me with all your heart." In other words, if a practitioner or recipient really wants to know God's mind on Reiki, He will tell them. Ultimately, by his Spirit, He will point individuals back to his Word that they have either rejected or were ignorant about it. Of course, some will say that God does not speak out specifically against Reiki in the Bible. It is true; He does not mention Reiki by name. But in Leviticus 19:31 and 20:6, He is very clear on prohibiting contact with spirits or mediums. When practitioners allow energy to flow through them, they are serving as a channel or medium. Again, someone could reason that Jesus opened himself up to have healing flow through Him. He did. However, He was clear that He was God, and his power came from God. Moreover, He never did anything to contradict what was already written in the Bible. The fact remains that God has multiple ways at his disposal to make the truth known. What is important is that individuals are honest in wanting to hear what God has to say. For some, they really do not want to know or care what God thinks. The notion of healing on demand is appealing. While it may benefit the recipient, it also strokes the healer. To meet needs that no one else has been able to meet is gratifying on many levels. Reiki speaks to one's sense of innate divinity to be able to provide healing.

Repenting and Renouncing

For those seeking a genuine relationship with God through Jesus Christ, it must be continually clarified that Reiki cannot be redeemed. Regardless of how it feels or makes others feel, the source of Reiki healing is distinct from the source of biblical healing. Moreover, when Reiki and biblical healing are compared side by side, there is no real comparison. Yes, individuals may talk about decreased anxiety or pain, and there are many anecdotal stories. But there really is no hard data to support real genuine miracles when using Reiki—no blind eyes or deaf ears opened, no medical reports to confirm disappearance of AIDS or cancer, no lame people walking, and no mute individuals talking. Let us suppose, there is hard data confirming "real" Reiki miracles in the future. The same reality exists today as it did during the time of Jesus' healing ministry. Every person that He healed eventually died. People who experience healing today will eventually die. What is next? Some practitioners and recipients believe that they will be reincarnated.

However, there is no support for reincarnation in the Bible regardless of how many have attempted to reinterpret scripture. What it does say in Hebrews 9:27 is that it is appointed for man once to die and afterwards face judgment. It is an interesting note that even Hindus have an understanding of "hell" which they feel people may inhabit between incarnations as a result of bad karma. Whether it is believed or not, the Bible teaches that all will stand before God. The emphasis will not be placed on healing of the mind or the body. The real question will be if the spirit was healed. That was certainly part of the purpose of Jesus' ministry on earth—to repair humanity's broken relationship with God by providing healing for the spirit. He also was destroying the works of the devil, to bring healing to whole people. Thus, for those snared by Reiki, the good news is that there is still time to repent. Repentance is a cease and desist order as well as a change in the way one thinks—the fruit of repentance is a change in the way one acts and lives. Individuals tell God that they are sorry, and they seek his forgiveness. Finally, they choose to live their lives in a way that pleases Him. That is where renouncing comes in. Reiki is rejected. Both practitioners and recipients must refuse to give or receive it. By God's power, the Reiki door is closed. Those seeking to leave Reiki must understand that a spiritual battle will take place. For some, the battle will be very intense. Prayer and fellowship with spiritually mature believers is essential The wonderful thing about repentance and renouncing is that it can open the door to a genuine relationship with God if the individual involved really desires to know God. Furthermore, there are gifts of the Spirit—like healing in addition to other gifts that God freely gives. However, what is more important than the gifts that God gives is having a relationship with Him through Jesus. After years of involvement in Reiki, Edward came to discover this truth. He did not arrive at this insight alone. In coming out of Reiki, he was aided by a discerning pastor and the Holy Spirit.

Journeying Out of Reiki

Prior to Edward's confrontation with God's truth concerning Reiki, he fully expected to be initiated into level three of Reiki. This would allow him to initiate others. He had already determined that the top person in the Reiki Alliance would facilitate that process. However, in hindsight, it was the Holy Spirit, which prompted Edward to invite Pastor Norris to speak at his church, and this meeting started Edward on his journey back to God. After his initial meeting with Pastor Norris, he admitted that internally a struggle was taking place. *"I was wrestling. The Lord wasn't going to continue to let me ride the fence. He doesn't tolerate other gods."* While having that knowledge, Edward still did not immediately let go of Reiki. *"I was convinced that I was still in my way, and [Pastor Norris] was in his way. But that's when the Holy Spirit started working on me."* Because he had at one time enjoyed fellowship with God, Edward was conversant in Scripture. He said that in reexamining the Bible, *"It wasn't as much me opening the book and hunting for things again as it was the Holy Spirit taking the pieces that I consciously was putting out my mind and putting them right back in the forefront where they burned."* The Scripture that the Holy Spirit spoke to his heart was in 1 Corinthians 10:21, "You can't drink of the cup of demons and drink the cup of the Lord. You can't eat of the table of demons and eat at the table of the Lord." This verse in particular represented a turn-around for him. He recounted, *"That grabbed hold of me so hard; it hurt so much when I realized where I had been and what I had done...."* He remembered his experience of partaking of the items belonging to the Hindu miracle worker who proclaimed he was God. He recognized, *"I had drank of the cup of demons; I had eaten at the table of demons and I knew it.... I had set Scriptures aside to follow this lust for power, for energy, [to] be the healer, to feel the power in my self...."* He said when that verse of Scripture *"brought it home, it brought such pain that I just wanted Pastor Norris to do it. Pastor Norris, get rid of this for me."* It was at that moment, he acknowledged, *"The Holy Spirit's conviction brought me to deep repentance"* (Harz, 34).

Pastor Norris recognized that the spirit that Edward had accessed for healing was not of God. Edward now recognized the truth. However, no attempt was made by Pastor Norris to lay hands on Edward to lift this influence off him. After the truth of the Bible penetrated his spirit and Edward experienced true godly sorrow, Pastor Norris wisely discerned, "[It's] *gone already. Now this is between you and the Lord."* Edward commented that, in the weeks that followed his initial repentance, he begged the Lord for cleansing. He maintained the *"process of inner-cleansing or sanctification"* was a process that took time, but he knew the *"Reiki demon was gone from the time of my repentance."* He later wrote that at the moment of repentance he immediately knew, *"I could not continue in the Reiki—a practice that opened the door and supported the entire New Age, old world, demonic practices"* (Harz, 35).

My Journey: In and Out of Reiki: A New Beginning 18

Ten years ago, I embarked on a journey that has altered my perception of healing, God's grace, and the universe outside my window. I did not recognize that the bondage of others could teach me so much about the God I thought I knew. While as researcher, I served as an observer; but in working for Virgil, I became a participant as well as an observer. I was allowed to see the effects of Reiki up close and personal. I saw how it changed an office and the people in it

My "stay" at Dr. Virgil Hartman's lasted approximately three years. In many ways, it felt like being transplanted into another world that challenged my theistic moorings. One aspect of Virgil that had intrigued me was a comment he made in reference to healing. He offered, "I believe that many of man's problems are spiritual." Therefore, while much of his early practice had been steeped in allopathic medicine, he saw the impact that spiritual health could have on the physical body. One of his major goals was getting people spiritually connected. I shared what I thought was a similar sentiment. True, I had serious misgivings about the people connected to the Healing Circle, but the group had pretty much disbanded. So initially, I looked forward to working with him and running the medical office. I also anticipated being able to facilitate strengthening his walk with God. I knew he would grow spiritually because he seemed very open to God.

My Journey: In and Out of Reiki: A New Beginning   199

Virgil was not the type who attended church every Sunday; but, initially, it seemed that he attended church once or twice of month. I was much encouraged because, at his insistence, we started every morning of work in prayer and frequently we prayed over the phone. I did most of the praying, but he was receptive none-the-less. He occasionally read the Bible, listened to Christian music I gave him, and he was deeply touched by the writings of Henri Nouwen, a well-known priest whose candor about struggles in his Christian walk had endeared him to many. I could see from the books that he had lying around that he had an interest in the "inspirational" writings of other religions, but I assumed that was part of Virgil's path and his attempt to be open-minded. The atmosphere of congeniality and acceptance between us continued for about a year.

Occasionally, Virgil struggled with hip problems and frequently went to holistic practitioners to have "body-work" done. He was open to various forms of healing if it relieved his symptoms. I articulated my concerns about the spirit behind the healing, but he generally smiled and participated in the experience. One day he asked me to pray for his hip. I agreed to do so but suggested he stop the alternative healing practices. I felt it would allow God the opportunity to touch his body. He smiled again. Two days later, he informed me that he had become certified in level one of Reiki. I felt sick because I instinctively knew that it would change the climate of the office.

Several weeks later, Virgil decided that the office needed to become more "clinically" oriented. Normally, I screened applicants and gave Virgil feedback as to the appropriateness of the candidate. We even prayed and asked God to send the right person; there was always agreement. However, this interview process was different. I interviewed Venus, and she appeared to have a good set of clinical skills. She was very interested in healing and spirituality. I queried her about what that really meant. When she told me that she had found God through automatic writing, a type of channeled writing, instinctively it reminded me of the eclectic spirituality of the Healing Circle. My reservations deepened when she said that she was a Reiki Master. I expressed my concerns to Virgil. I lauded her clinical abilities but noted concerns about the direction the spiritual climate of the office would take. He listened attentively and said he would let me know. Within a few days, he informed me that he had already called Venus and she would start soon. He mumbled something about expecting my full support and reminded me that this was his practice.

As it worked out, I was to do the morning shift, and she would do the afternoon shift. However, there were times that our schedules overlapped. While she was animated and friendly, I was cool and professional. I knew that things around me were changing. She was given the task of reviving the defunct Healing Circle, and she did it with gladness.

The times that Virgil and I prayed together for the office became infrequent. Even when I arrived earlier, he made it a point to be very busy in the morning. When we did pray, I sensed his discomfort and could literally feel him pull his hands away as I prayed. Eventually, we stopped praying all together.

One member of my staff was very vocal about her Christian faith, and she constantly talked about the goodness of God. This had never been a problem, and patients seemed to enjoy knowing that someone was saying a prayer for them. Virgil informed me directly that staff should not be vocal about their Christian beliefs as it might offend patients who were of other faiths. I asked how he could be a Christian interested in healing and yet not want Jesus discussed. He talked about the legitimacy of all spiritual paths. Thus, the universe, Reiki, and ideologies from the East were frequently discussed.

Not long after Venus came, I was informed in a staff meeting that Reiki would be made available to the patients. The decision had already been made. Virgil explained to me that the office was changing in ways I might not understand. I found out that one of the first Reiki patients was a colicky newborn. I was horrified, and I really wanted to quit. But somehow, at that point, I felt no release to just quit. One could argue that I had judged Reiki without experiencing it for myself, but I could see the changes in Virgil early on. If it caused individuals to back away from Jesus, terminate prayer, and fall away from church, it could not be healing based in the God of the Bible.

What I noticed most when the practice of Reiki entered the office was the sudden increase in patient mortality and transfer rates. Some who had been patients for years were suddenly leaving. As a physician, Virgil had enjoyed a very low patient mortality and hospitalization rate. Part of this was due to his strong belief in preventative medicine and early diagnosis. The first year I was there, prior to Reiki, maybe one or two patients died a year. Over the next two years, at least 20 patients died. Granted some of them were older with chronic diseases, so that was to be expected. However, what was surprising, was the suddenness of some patients' demise and the virulence of the diseases. What was most noticeable was the unexplainable elevated incidence of patients with cancers that defied intervention. There were already a few patients who had slow-growing cancers. Generally, the patients lingered for several years before dying. Moreover, their bodies responded to varying levels of intervention. However, I recognized that often cancers were asymptomatic and appeared suddenly. That had not been my initial experience, nor was it typical of the office in general.

Lab work began to come back with high biomarkers, substances found in the blood, body fluids, or tissues. A high level of biomarker could sometimes indicate the presence of cancer. One such biomarker was a Prostate Specific Antigen (PSA) reading used to screen for prostate cancer. Values that ranged between $0.1\mu g/L$-$4.0\mu g/L$ were considered average, according to the lab we used. However, on a monthly basis, three to four labs came back with values above the 4.0 level. The staff would comment about the "high labs" and Dr. Hartman's need to talk to these patients. This was not to suggest that scores of men developed prostate cancer. It was just a noticeable change in the elevation levels.

Another biomarker known as Carcinogenic Embryonic Antigen (CEA) was used to monitor the treatment of colorectal, breast, lung, and pancreatic malignancies. While it was not recommended as a diagnostic screening test, the test was occasionally given if symptoms hinted at cancer. The reference range was 0-4μg/L and the borderline range was 4-10μg/L. Two otherwise reasonably healthy patients were referred to specialists for exertional dyspnea, which indicated difficulty in breathing. One developed lung cancer. Although that patient did not smoke, was not exposed to smoke or known toxins, and had no family history of cancer, the patient was diagnosed with Stage IV cancer and was dead within three months. A second patient around a similar time was sent to a specialist and a CEA test was given. The CEA level was above 300—far above even the borderline level. The patient was dead within one month although, outside of the shortness of breath, there were no other symptoms contributing to the diagnosis.

While neither of these patients was directly treated with Reiki, it was now practiced in the office. Reiki energy does have a presence, and while supporters could argue that Reiki was a harmless intelligent energy, I had already witnessed the spiritual impact it had on Virgil's relationship to God. When I expressed my shock and sadness to Venus over the suddenness of one death, she flatly responded that sometimes the planet needed to cleanse itself.

While I do not know for certain what caused their sudden untimely demise or the sudden deaths of other patients whose check-ups indicated they were doing well, I know that the atmosphere of the office changed quickly and not in a positive manner. Anderson and Ameling (2000) referenced a case study in which a dying woman was being sent distant Reiki for several months for a long-term disease. What stood out was the following comment made by the Reiki practitioner when the patient suddenly developed cancer, "Her newly discovered breast cancer and the speed of its metastases were astonishing" (28). The point is that there could be a possible connection between Reiki being sent at a distance and the rapid spread of cancer although it was not perceived as such. I know there are many anecdotal stories where alleged cancers have been sent into remission. I can only share what my personal experience has been. Did some people seem to benefit from Reiki? I am sure they believed they did. However, there was no mechanism or desire to track Reiki's effects over time. What seemed to matter most was if patients felt better.

As the patient base lessened, insurance reimbursements decreased, and individuals representing varying healing arts came seeking space on the third level, I knew my time to leave was imminent. Virgil had made a clear choice about what he felt healing represented; it was about getting people spiritually connected. However, in substance, it bore no reflection to the healing power of the God I knew. I left Virgil as I had found him, "on his path." However, the seeds were sown. Only God in his way and in his time could give the increase.

In time, I grew to appreciate the experience. God had allowed me to gain insight into the world that existed outside my window—a world I know I would have never ventured towards. While in that world, I frequently felt varying levels of pain and disgust. The practices were wrong. They had missed the mark, and I thought that eventually each would feel some level of divine wrath—I was sure of it. That was the God I thought I knew. However, in time, he allowed me to see that while He is a God that will ultimately judge all sin; He is still a God of grace and mercy. He is the one who determines when mercy has run its course. It is not my call.

He showed me the tentative nature of my love for others. When Virgil initially seemed to respond to God's counsel in me, I cared about him and prayed for him daily. However, when he began to move in the opposite direction, I backed away. I was tolerant, but there was no heart-felt agape love—something so critical in counseling individuals who have been snared by Reiki. The Holy Spirit reminded me that without agape love, I had nothing to offer of any eternal value. Agape love did not develop overnight; it took time and true humility to develop God's love. It required dying to self and my desire for things to "be right" in my timing. As I confessed the impatience of my own heart, He began to adjust my attitude.

I realized that God desired that I love what He loved and hate what he hated. He hated sin, not people. My attitude did not change about Reiki or any of the other practices that took place. It was not the healing of the Bible. Nevertheless, my attitude slowly changed about the people. They were in bondage and needed to be free. However, that would never happen if no one interceded on the behalf of the practitioners or the recipients. It would never happen if the Jesus I knew they needed to connect with was only conditionally reflected in me.

Thus, the experience has been transformative. It has given me a new revelation of God; He has clarified what was important to him. People, the souls of people, are still very important to him. He has made it clear to me that He died to heal each practitioner, and until Jesus returns, there is still hope. Each one of them may still respond to his call. My goal is simply to tell them the truth in love and reflect his image. He had allowed me to see that each practitioner was a seeker. They thought they had made the ultimate connection. I knew differently because I had the experience of hearing his voice early, so I would not follow other voices. I had the opportunity to see and experience genuine biblical healing, so I could identify a counterfeit. It was simply grace. I have left this seven-year journey assured that if Virgil and the others would seek God with their whole hearts, eventually they would find him. My task was to intercede for them and where possible, love them into wholeness. That was my new beginning—seeing them through my Father's eyes. I also left the experience having learned something from the Reiki practitioners. Although the source of the healing was not the power that Jesus accessed, they understood something that even many Christians have yet to grasp—physical healing is still for today.

References Cited

Alandydy, Patricia and Kristen Alandydy. 1999. Performance brief: Using Reiki to support surgical patients. *Journal of Nursing Care Quality* 13: 89-91.

Ameling, Ann and Margaret Povilonis. 2001. Spirituality meaning, mental health and nursing. *Alternative Complementary Therapies* (April): 15-20.

Anderson, Norman. 1984. *Christianity and world religions: The challenge of pluralism*. Downers Grove: Inter-Varsity Press.

Ankerberg, John and John Weldon. 1991. *Can you trust your doctor?* Brentwood: Wolgemuth & Hyatt Publishers, Inc.

_____. 1996. *Encyclopedia of New Age beliefs*. Eugene: Harvest House Publishers.

Ashworth, David. 2001. *Dancing with the devil as you channel light: Survival guide for healers and therapists*. Bath, United Kingdom: Crucible Publishers.

Assefin, P., A. Bogart, J. Goldberg, D. Buchwald. 2008. Reiki for the treatment of Fibromyalgia: A randomized control trial. *Journal of Complementary and Alternative Medicine*. 14(9):1115-22.

Barnett, Libby and Maggie Chambers. 1996. *Reiki energy medicine: Bringing healing touch into home, hospital, and hospice*. Rochester: Healing Arts Press.

Beasley-Murray, G. R. 1992. Soul care in the ministry of Jesus. *Canadian Journal of the Evangelical Theological Society* 85.01: 19-30.

Berling, Judith A. 1982. Taoism, or the way. *Focus on Asian Studies*. No.1: 9-11, available from *Focus on Asian Studies*, <http:www.askasia.org> (accessed 22 December 2004).

Biali, Susan. 2002. The energy of Reiki: Working on the premise that unobstructed energy flow is associated with general health and well-being, Dr. Susan Biali investigates how Reiki treats more than physical body. *Medical Post* 38: no. 33: 25-26.

Birnbaum, Raoul. 1979. *The healing Buddha*. Boulder: Shambhala Publications, Inc.
Boltz, William G. 1993. "Lao tzu Tao te ching". *In early Chinese texts: A bibliographic guide*, ed. Michael Loewe. 269-92 Berkley: University of California, Institute of East Asian Studies.
Borgen, Peder. 1981. Miracles of healing in the New Testament. *Studia Thelogica* 35 (1) 91-106
Briones, Maricris. 2002. Spiritual side effects. *Science and Spirit*.
Bucholtz, R.A. 1996. *The Use of Reiki therapy in the treatment of pain in rheumatoid arthritis pain*. Unpublished Masters Thesis, University of Wisconsin.
Bullock, Marlene. 1997. Reiki: A complementary therapy for life. *American Journal of Hospital and Palliative Care* 14 (1): 31-33.
Carol. 2009. SPCDC: Spiritual Warfare BBS. Available from www.http://saintpiocenter.org. Internet; accessed 09 March 2010.
Chan, Alan. 2002. Laozi. *"The Stanford encyclopedia of philosophy"*. (Spring 2002 Edition). Edward N. Zalta. ed. [e-journal] http://plato.stanford,edu/archives/spr2002/entries/laozi/.
Chang, Lit-Sen. 1999. *Asia's religions: Christianity's momentous encounter with paganism*. Phillisburg: P & R Publishing.
Chang, Sung Ok. 2001. Meaning of ki related to touch in caring. *Holistic Nursing Practice* 16 (1): 73-84.
Chung, Jun Ki. 1997. Taoism in Christian perspective. *Journal of Interdisciplinary Studies* no. 1-2: 173-178, Available from *First Search*, <http:www.firstsearch.org> [accessed 11 December 2004].
Collie, El. 1995. "Kundalini signs and symptoms." *Shared Transformation online*. Available from http://www.elcollie.com/st.st.html/ (accessed 3 March 2005).
Courcey, Kevin. 2000. Therapeutic touch: "A comprehensive overview of the history, practice, and research," database on-line *Philadelphia Association for Critical Thinking*. Available from www.phact.org/e/tt/ (accessed 3 March, 2002).
Davis, Freddy. 2006. What is far eastern thought? Available from www.marketfaith.org (accessed 6 February 2010).
Eckman, James. 2006. *The truth about worldviews: A biblical understanding of worldview alternatives*. Wheaton: Evangelical Training Association.
Ellyard, Lawrence. 2004. *Reiki healer: A complete guide to an ancient healing art*. Twin Lakes: Lotus Press.
Engebretson, J. and D.W. Wardell. 1977. Biological correlates of Reiki touch healing.
Journal of Advanced Nursing 33(4): 439-445.

_____. 2002. Experience of a Reiki session. *Alternative Therapies* 8: no. 2: 48-53.

Epperly, Bruce. 2001. *God's touch: Faith, wholeness, and the healing miracles of Jesus*. Louisville: Westminister John Knox Press.

Ernst, E., M.S, Lee, H. Pittler. Effects of Reiki in clinical practice: A systematic review of randomized trials. *Journal of Clinical Practice* 62: 947-954.

Feng, Gia-Gu and Jane English. 1989 and 1972, *Tao te ching*, trans, Feng and English, with a foreword by Jacob Needleman. New York: Ballentine Books.

Ferguson, Everett. 1975. Laying on of hands: Its significance in ordination. *Journal of Theological Studies*, n. s., 26: 1-12.

Fish, Sharon. 1996.Therapeutic touch: Healing science a psychic midwife. *Christian Research Journal* (Summer): 6.

Flusser, David. 1957. Healing through the laying on of hands in a Dead Sea scroll. *Israel Exploration* 7 no. 2: 107-108.

Gaebelein, Frank E. Ed. 1989-1998. *The expositors Bible commentary*. Zondervan Reference Software. (Version 2.6) [CD-ROM] The Zondervan Corporation.

Gallob, Robin. 2003. Reiki: A supportive therapy in nursing practice and self-care for nurses. *Journal of the New York State Nurses Association* (Spring/Summer): 9-13.

Gerhardsson, Birger. 1979. *The mighty acts of Jesus according to Matthew*. Lund: Publications of the Royal Society of Letters at Lund: Monographs (ACTA).

Greenwell, Bonnie. 1988. *Energies of transformation: A guide to the Kundalini process*. Valenica: Shakti River Press.

Grof, Stanislav and Christina Grof. ed. 1989. *Spiritual emergency: When personal transformation becomes a crisis*. New York: Jeremy P. Tarcher/Putman.

Gumprecht, Jane. 1988. *New Age health care: Holy or holistic*. Orange County: Promise Publishing Company.

Halverson, Dean. ed. 1996. *The compact guide to world religions*. Minneapolis: Bethany House Publishers.

Hargreaves, Cecil. 1964. *The miracles of Jesus*. Park Town: The Christian Literature Society.

Harris, Darryl. 1998. The mystery and meaning of Reiki. B.S.N honors thesis, University of Western Sydney Nepean: School of Health & Nursing.

Harrison, Paul. 1987. Buddhism: A religion of revelation after all? *Numen* 34.02: 256-264.

Harz, E.S. 1998. *The Reiki danger: Healing that harms*. United States.

Heil, John Paul. 1979. Significant aspects of the healing miracles in Matthew. *The Catholic Biblical Quarterly* 41: 274-287

Henry, Carl. 1992. Reflections on the kingdom of God. *Journal of the Evangelical Theological Society* 35 1: 39-49.

Hiers, Richard H. 1986. Kingdom of God. *Interpretation* 40 no. 3: 313.

Hendricks, Robert B. 1989. *Tao te ching.* trans. Robert Hendricks. New York: Vintage Books.

Jikai, and Jihu. 2000. "Tendai Buddhism for Americans": Chap. IV. ed. Bob Williams. *Tendai*-us online. Available from <http<://www.tendai-us.org 1&for a 6.html> (accessed 21 November 2004).

Jiko, Hazama, 1987. The characteristics of Japanese Tendai. *Japanese Journal of Religious Studies* 14/2–3: 101-112.

Johnston, George. 1960. Soul care in the ministry of Jesus. *Canadian Journal of Theology* 6 no. 1: 25-30.

Kelly, Maureen J. 2000. *Reiki and the healing Buddha.* Twin Lakes: Lotus Press.

Kallas, James. 1961. *The significance of the synoptic miracles.* London: The Talbot Press.

Keathley, Hampton. 2004. The miracles of Jesus. *Bible.org online.* Home page online. Available from http://www.bible.org (accessed 28 September 2004).

Kelsey, Morton K. 1995. *Healing and Christianity: A classic study.* Minneapolis: Augsburg.

Kelner, M.J., H. Boon, B. Wellman, and S. Welsh. 2002. Complementary and alternative groups contemplate the need for effectiveness safety and cost-effectiveness research. *Complementary Therapies in Medicine* 235-239.

Kelner, M. and B. Wellmen. 1997. Who seeks alternative healthcare: A profile of the users of five modes of treatment. *Journal of Alternative and Complementary Medicine* 3:2: 127-140.

Kennedy, Pat. 2001. Working with survivors of torture in Sarajevo with Reiki. *Complementary Therapies in Nursing and Midwifery* 7(1): 4-7.

Khoo, Kay Keng. 1998. The Tao and the Logos: Lao Tzu and the Gospel of John. *International Review of Mission.* 87.344: 77- 80.

Koch, Kurt E. 1994. *Christian counseling and occultism.* Grand Rapids: Kregel Publications.

Kohn, Livia. 1993. Taoist scriptures as mirrored in Xiaodaolun. *Taoist Resources* 4 no. 1: 47-69.

Kraiss, Wayne E. 1983. Anointing with oil and laying on of hands. In *Conference on the Holy Spirit Digest.* ed. Gwen Jones, 281-285. Springfield: Gospel Publishing House

Krieger, Dolores. 1975. Therapeutic Touch: The imprimatur of nursing.

American Journal of Nursing 75: 784-787.

_____.1979. *The Therapeutic Touch: How to use your hands to help or heal*. New York: Simon & Schuster.

_____.1993. *Accepting Your Power to Heal*. Santa Fe: Bear and Company.

Lai, Whalen W. 1987. Why the lotus sutra: On the historic significance of Tendai. *Japanese Journal of religious Studies* 14/2- 3: 83-99.

Lalleman, Pieter J. 1997. Healing by a mere touch as a Christian concept. *Tyndale Bulletin* 48.2: 355-361.

Lardie, Debra. 2000. *Concise dictionary of the occult and New Age*. Paul Ingram and Dan Lioy. ed. Grand Rapids: Kregel Publications.

Levine, Myra E. 1975. "Letter to the Editor". *American Journal of Nursing* (August 1975): 1383.

Leffel, Jim. 1994. "Understanding Basic Beliefs". *Xenos* online. Home page online. Available from http://www.xenos.org/essays/understanding-basic-beliefs

Loos, V.D. 1965. *The Miracles of Jesus*. Leiden: Novum Testamentum Supplements

Lubeck, Walter, Frank Arjava Petter and William Lee Rand. 2001. *The Spirit of Reiki: The Complete Handbook of the Reiki System*. Twin Lakes: Lotus Press.

Mainfort, Donald. 2004. The physician-shaman: Early origins of traditional Chinese medicine. *Skeptic* 11 no.1: 36-39.

Mair, Victor. 1990. *Tao te ching: The classic book of integrity and the way*. trans. Victor Mair. New York: Bantam Books.

Mansour, A.A., M. Beuche, G. Lang, and A. Lewis. 1999. A study to test the effectiveness of placebo Reiki standardization procedures developed for a planned Reiki efficacy study. *Journal of Alternative Complementary Medicine* 5 (3): 153-164.

Mattingly, Keith. 2001. The significance of Joshua's reception of the laying on of hands in Numbers 27: 12-23. *Andrews University Seminary Studies* 39, no. 2: 191-208.

McClenton, R. 2005. Spirits of a lesser god: A critical examination of Reiki and Christ-centered healing. PhD diss,. Trinity Theological Seminary in cooperation with the University of Liverpool. Ann Arbor. Proquest

McClenton, Rhonda. 2005. *Spirits of a lesser god: A critical examination of Reiki and Christ-centered healing*. Boca Raton: Dissertation.com

Miles, Pamela. 2003. Research letter: A report on the use of Reiki for HIV-related pain and anxiety. *Alternative Therapies* 9 no. 2: 36.

_____. 2003. Pamela Miles: Reiki Vibrational healing. Interview by Bonnie Horrigan. *Alternative Therapies* no. 4: 75-83.

Miles, Pamela and Gala True. 2003. Reiki: Review of a biofield therapy history, theory, practice and research. *Alternative Therapies* (Mar., Apr.): 62-71.
Miller, Elliott. 1992. The Christian energetic medicine, and New Age paranoia. *Christian Research Journal* (Winter): 24-27.
Miller, James. 2001. Envisioning the Daoist body in the economy of cosmic power. *Daedalus*, 130: 4 [journal on-line] Available from *Questia*, http://www.questia.com.
Miller, Roland. 1991. Christ the healer. *Consensus* 17 no.2: 20-32.
Mills, Jeri. 2001. *Tapestry of healing: Where Reiki and medicine intertwine.* Alto: White Sage Press.
Ming, Zhu. 2001. *The medical classic of the yellow emperor.* trans. Ming Zhu. Beijing: Foreign Languages Press.
Mitchell, Stephen. 1988. *Tao te ching*, trans. Stephen Miller. New York: Harper Collins Publishers.
Moss, Thelma. 1974. *The probability of the impossible: Scientific discoveries and explanations of the psychic world.* New York: New American Library.
Mote, Frederick. 1971. *Intellectual foundations of China.* New York: Alfred Knopf.
Neild-Anderson, Leslie and Ann Ameling. 2000. The empowering nature of Reiki as a complementary therapy. *Holistic Nursing Practice.* 14: (3) 21-29.
Ni, Hua-Ching. 1979. *The complete works of Lao Tzu: Tao the ching and hua hu ching.* trans. Hua-Ching Ni. Santa Monica: Seven Star Communications.
O'Mathuna, Donal. 2001. *Therapeutic touch and human energy field therapies: A realistic evaluation* (unpublished work) p. 37.
Pantheist Association for Nature. 1998. A kaleidoscopic collection of quotations to complement a Pantheistic outlook. http://home.utm.net/pan (accessed 25 February 2010).
Park, O'Hyan. 1975. Chinese religion and the religions of China. *Perspectives in Religious Studies* 2 (Fall): 159-190.
Petter, Frank Arjava. 1997. *Reiki Fire.* Twin Lakes: Lotus Light Publications.
_____. 1999. *Reiki: The legacy of Dr. Usui.* Twin Lakes: Lotus Light.
Rambelli, Fabio. 2002. The ritual world of Buddhist Shinto. *Japanese Journal of Religious Studies* 29/3-4: 265-297.
Rand, William Lee. *Becoming a Reiki Master.* The International Center for Reiki Training [database online], Available from <http://www.reikiorg/reikinews/reiki3. html.>
Reisser, Paul, Teri Reisser and John Weldon. 1988. *New Age medicine: A Christian perspective on holistic health.* Chattanooga: Global Publishers.

Reisser, Paul, Dale Mabe and Robert Velarde. 2001. *Examining alternative medicine: An inside look at the benefits and risks*. Downers Grove: Intervarsity Press.

Reisser, Paul, Dale Mabe and Robert Velarde. 2001. *Examining alternative medicine: An inside look at the benefits and risks*. Downers Grove: Intervarsity Press.

Remus, Harold. 1977. *Jesus the healer*. Cambridge: Cambridge University Press.

Rosa, L., E. Rosa, L. Sarner, S. Barrett, MD. 1998. A closer look at Therapeutic Touch. *JAMA* 297: 1005-1010.

Russell, Terence C. 1990. Chen Tuan's veneration of the *Dharma*: A study in hagiographic modification. *Taoist Resources* 2.01: 54-72.

Sansom, M.C. 1983. Laying on of hands in the Old Testament. *Expository Times*, 94: 323-326.

Saso, Michael. 1987. Kuden: the oral Hermeneutics of Tendai Tantric Buddhism. *Japanese Journal of Religious Studies*. 14/2 – 3: 235-246. .

Saucy, Mark. 1997. Kingdom of God and the teaching of Jesus: In twentieth century theology. Nashville. W Publishing Group.

Sawyer, Jeanette. 1998. The first Reiki practitioner in our OR. *Association of Operating Room Nurses Journal* 67:3: 674-674.

Schmehr, Robert. 2003. Enhancing the treatment of HIV/AIDS with Reiki training and treatment. *Alternative Therapies* 9 no. 2: 120-121.

Schmidt, Laurie. 2009. Reiki allows me to continue the healing ministry of Jesus. *National Catholic Reporter.*[journal on line] available from ncronline.org/news/spirituality/reiki-allows-me-continue-healing-ministry-jesus

Shore, Adina. 2001. Long-Term effects of Energetic healing on symptoms of psychological depression and self-perceived stress. *Alternative Therapies in Health and Medicine* 10 no. 3: 42-48 Available from http://proquest.umi (accessed 22 June 2004).

Sire, James W. 2009 *The universe next door*. Downers Grove: InterVarsity Press.

Skeen, James, 2002. Theosophy: A historical analysis and refutation. *Quodilibet Journal*. 4 no. 2-3 [journal on-line] available from www.quodlibet.net/articles/skeen.theosophy.shtml

So, Pui Shan, Y. Jiang, Y.Qin. 2008. Touch therapies for pain relief in adults. *Cochrane Database of Systematic Reviews*. 4. Available from http://mrw.interscience.wiley.com (accessed 22 February 2010).

Stahlman, Jack. "A brief history of Therapeutic Touch." 2000. Edited by B. Scheiber and C. Selby. *Therapeutic Touch*. New York: Prometheus Books.

Stein, Diane. 1995. *Essential Reiki: A complete guide to an ancient healing art*. California: The Crossing Press, Inc.

Stiene, Bronwen and Frans. 2003. *The Reiki sourcebook*. New York: John Hunt Publishing.
Sullivan, Frances A. 1994. The laying on of hands in Christian tradition. *Spirit andRenewal* 42-54.
Sunde, Merle. 1998. *Reiki: Universal life force energy.* A.R.T. Productions. 35 min. Videocasette.
Thornton, L. M. 1996. Effects of energetic science healing on female nursing students. *Rogerian Science News* (Spring) 13–14 (Winter): 14-15.
Tipei, John F. 2000. The function of the laying on of hands in the Old Testament. *Journal of the European Pentecostal Theological Association* 20: 93-115.
Tirth, Shivom Swami. 1997. *A guide to Shaktipat*. New York: Sparrow Bush.
Tucker, Mary. 1998. Religion dimensions of Confucianism: Cosmology and cultivation. *Philosophy East and West* no. 1: 5-45 [journal on-line] Available from *Questia*, http://www.questia.com.
Twelftree, Graham H. 1999. *Jesus: The miracle worker*. Downers Grove: Intervarsity Press.
United States Conference of Catholic Bishops. 2009. Guidelines for evaluating Reiki. Internet on-line. Available from http://www.usccb.org/doctrine/publications.shtml (accessed 8 March 2010).
Vennells, David F. 2004. *Reiki mastery*. New York: John Hunt Publishing.
Wallis, Ian G. 1992. Christ's continuing ministry of healing. *The Expository Times* 104: 42-45.
Ward, C.A. 1989. *Altered States of Consciousness and mental health: A cross-cultural perspective*. Newbury Park: Sage
Waters, C.J. 2002. Healing in the context of ministry. *The Expository Times* 113 no. 11: 372-374.
Warrington, Keith. 2000. *Jesus the healer: Paradigm or unique phenomenon*. Waynesboro: Paternoster Publishing.
Wetzel, Wendy. 1989. Reiki healing: A Physiologic Perspective. *Journal of Holistic Nursing no. 7*: 47-53.
Whelan, Kathleen and Gracie Wishnia. 2003. Reiki therapy: The benefits to a nurse/Reiki practitioner. *Holistic Nursing Practice* 17 (4): 209-217.
Whitsitt, Terry. 1998. Reiki Therapy. *Journal of Christian Nursing* 15 no.1: 12-13.
Wirth, Daniel P., Joseph T. Richardson and William S. Erdelman. 1996. Wound healing and complementary therapies: A review. *The Journal of Alternative and Complementary Medicine* 2 no. 4: 493-502.
Zodhiates, Spiros, ed. 1996. *The Hebrew-Greek key study Bible*. Chattanooga: AMG Publishers.

Index

A
absentee healing 33, 34
Acupuncture 14
altered states of consciousness 50, 164, 169, 171
alternative medicine 19, 95
Ameling, Ann 43, 90, 154, 202
Anderson, Sir Norman 43, 54, 90, 154, 202, 205, 210
Ankerberg, John 24, 84, 108, 169, 171, 172, 179
Ashworth, David 155, 167, 168,
assessment 48, 54, 63, 76, 77, 85, 88, 160, 179
astral projection 33, 160, 164
astral travel 169
atman 72
attunements 19, 20, 31, 32, 35, 43-47, 176
Authority Over Death 135

B
Barnett and Chambers 90, 91, 92
Bearheart 33, 34, 165, 180, 182, 186
Beasley-Murray, G.R. 126
Berling, Judith 63
biblical worldview 30, 70, 146, 147
biofields 49
Biofield Therapy 23, 49
blind man 54, 120, 121, 138
Bodisattvas 47
Book of Changes 51

Borgen, Peder 123
born again 107, 113
born-again Christians 157
Brahman 72
Bucholtz, R.A. 89
Buddha 37, 38, 40, 41, 42, 44, 45, 46, 49, 53, 182
Buddhist 37-41, 43, 44, 46, 47, 50, 68, 69, 82, 90, 92, 160
Buddhist worldview 46
Bullock, Marlene 89, 91

C
Calvin, John 137
Catholic Church 157, 158
Centering 76
chakra 18, 36, 154, 156, 180
chakra system 154, 156
Chang, Lit-Sen 50, 53, 64
channel 19, 20, 26, 31, 33, 43, 68, 108, 161, 164, 194, 205
Chi 29, 44, 50, 51, 52, 54, 55, 58, 60, 61, 65, 67, 70
Christianity 53, 54, 64, 81, 93, 121, 137, 146, 147, 160, 162, 173, 177, 178, 182, 193, 205, 206, 208
Chuang Tzu 53
Chung, Jun Ki 63, 206
clairvoyance 36, 84, 164, 172, 177
compassion 92, 122, 123, 136, 142, 144, 169, 193, 194
conferral of the Holy Spirit 120

Confucism 47
Creator 53, 61, 64, 65, 66, 70, 74, 133, 146, 148, 175, 190
crippled woman 140, 185
cross 113, 141, 143, 160, 212
crown 20, 36, 169

D

Dancing with the Devil: Survival for Healers and Therapists 155
danger 19, 109, 149, 158, 163, 167, 207
Dao 55, 56, 58, 61, 62, 63
Davis, Freddy 72, 148, 206
death 73, 91, 102, 109, 110, 111, 136, 142, 143, 148, 187, 188, 202
deception 159. 192
deceptions 155
deity 136, 139
demon 27, 28, 104, 109, 141, 162, 164, 178, 197
depression 35, 91, 92, 93, 94, 211
Dharma 40, 41, 42, 43, 44, 46, 48, 211
discipleship 144
divination 29, 41, 51, 63
dynamis 131, 134

E

Eckman, James 71, 206
effectiveness 95, 97, 153, 163, 208, 209
Ellyard, Lawrence 32, 36, 40, 41, 42, 46, 47, 206
energeia 134
energy 14, 19, 20, 22, 26-39, 43, 45-52, 54, 55, 57, 58, 60, 61, 62, 65, 66, 67, 70, 71, 76-80, 83, 84, 85, 87, 90, 91, 95, 96, 108, 110, 131, 134, 144, 145, 153-155, 159-162, 164, 167-170, 173-180, 183, 186, 188, 194, 197, 202, 205, 210, 212
energy fields 49, 51, 83
Engebretson and Wardell 88, 89, 91, 95, 154, 164, 206
Enlightenment 37, 38
Estabany, Oskar 82
eternity 144, 148, 185, 189
exorcisms 124, 125
exsousia 142

F

faith 13, 18, 24, 41, 85, 104, 105, 106, 111, 113, 123, 124, 131, 132, 133, 134, 135, 136, 140, 143, 144, 149, 157, 159, 162, 163, 185, 190, 200
Fish, Sharon 77, 80, 83, 86, 207
five elements 52, 53, 54, 55
forgiveness of sins 123, 125, 132, 133
Frank Lloyd Wright 73
Fruit of Reiki 174

G

Gallob, Robin 90, 97, 154, 207
Gerhardsson, Birger 132, 207
gifts of the Spirit 113, 196
God 13, 14, 15, 16, 17, 18, 20, 21, 22, 23, 29, 33, 40, 45, 53, 62, 63, 64, 66, 70, 71, 72, 73, 74, 91, 101, 104, 105, 106, 107, 108, 111-118, 121-127, 130-133, 135, 136, 138-149, 153, 158-166, 172-179, 183-204, 207, 208, 211
Golden, Susan 92
Guidelines for Evaluating Reiki 157

H

harm 26, 97, 98, 153, 154, 155, 161, 162, 163, 166, 167, 171, 173, 178, 191
Harrison, Paul 74, 207
healing energies 50
healing energy 19, 20, 26, 38, 39, 55, 58, 60, 61, 66, 67, 70, 90, 159, 186
Hearing and Speech-Impaired Man 137
Hemorrhaging Woman 133
Hendricks, Robert G. 61, 208
Higher Self 29
Hinduism 71, 81, 164, 177
HIV/AIDS 24, 94
Holy Spirit 21, 70, 104, 111-113, 120, 127, 134, 147, 159, 169, 176, 178, 183-186, 188-190, 192, 196, 197, 203, 208
human energy field 77, 80, 83, 85, 210

I

idolatry 54, 64, 158

imbalance 52, 53
initiation 19, 20, 32, 33, 43, 44, 45, 94, 123, 138, 167, 173, 179
initiation rituals 43, 44
invisible energy 54

J

Jarius' Daughter 135
Jesus 14, 18, 23, 24, 29, 37, 62, 64, 65, 66, 70, 82, 91, 103, 106–113, 115, 118–145, 147, 158, 159, 161, 162, 163, 166, 173–178, 180, 183–186, 188–196, 200, 201, 204, 205, 207, 208, 209, 211, 212
Journal of Christian Nursing 155, 212
Journal of the American Medical Association 85
Judaism 123, 146, 147
Judeo-Christian 93, 174, 189
jumons 43

K

kanjo 43, 44
Kelsey, Morton T. 144, 208
Khoo, Kay Keng 62, 63, 208
Ki 29, 39, 44, 49, 50, 51, 54, 55, 58, 63, 70, 90, 206
kingdom of God 122, 123, 124, 125, 126, 127, 130, 132, 138, 141, 143, 208
Kohn, Livia 69, 208
kotodamas 43
Krieger, Dolores 75, 76, 77, 78, 80, 81, 82, 83, 84, 208
kundalini 156
Kundalini Awakening 167–170, 173
Kundalini Reiki 168. *See* Kundalini Awakening
Kunz, Dora 76, 80, 81, 82, 83, 84
Kushu Shinren 46

L

Lao Tzu 53, 55, 60, 62, 208, 210
laying-on of hands 23, 37, 44, 45, 47, 48, 75, 80, 82, 83, 101, 114–121, 125, 130, 131, 138, 142–144, 153, 156, 167, 190, 191

Leadbeater, Charles 81, 82, 167
level one 27, 31–34, 94, 199
level three 34, 196
level two 33, 34, 181
life energy 39, 83, 91, 108
Light 140, 210
Light of the World 140
Loos, V.D. 121, 123, 132, 133, 137, 141, 209
Lotus Sutra 41, 46

M

magic 25, 54, 55, 121
Mainfort, Donald 51, 52, 54, 55, 209
mandalas 41, 42, 47
mantra 34, 36, 43, 44, 76
massage 26, 28, 35, 176
material reality 72, 148
Mattingly, Keith 117, 209
maya 71
meditation 25, 41, 42, 46, 58, 94, 96, 160, 179
medium(s) 29, 133, 194
mediumship 30, 86
mental illness 172
Messiah 123, 124, 125, 133, 142
Miles, Pamela 23, 24, 40, 49, 50, 55, 60, 68, 90, 96, 154, 183, 209, 210
miracles 38, 113, 121, 123, 124, 126, 127, 128, 137, 143, 176, 195, 207, 208
miracles of Jesus 121, 122, 126, 129, 131, 209
Miracles of Jesus, The 121, 122, 129, 131, 209
Mitchell, Stephen 59
modulation 76, 77
monism 47
mudras 34, 41–43, 47

N

nature 23, 41, 46, 52, 53, 56, 57, 59, 61, 63, 65, 71–74, 93, 95, 96, 125, 137, 148, 154, 161, 172, 190, 191, 203, 210
Nei Ching 51
New Age 23, 197, 205, 207, 209, 210

New Testament 23, 108, 109, 110, 119, 120, 123, 125, 126, 138, 147, 206
Nield-Anderson 43, 90, 154
non-dual primordial Chi 50, 55

O
obedience 53, 63, 116, 117, 140, 158, 191
occult 18, 19, 23, 29, 30, 48, 51, 54, 55, 80, 81, 83, 84, 86, 155, 156, 159, 160, 164, 165, 166, 167, 169, 171, 172, 173, 174, 175, 177, 179, 183, 189, 190, 193, 209
occult bondage 165, 172, 173, 183
occult subjugation 165
Old Testament 23, 108, 115, 116, 117, 118, 119, 125, 126, 147, 211, 212
O'Mathuna, Dónal 51, 143, 154, 168, 210

P
pantheism 47, 71, 72
Pantheist Association for Nature 73, 74, 210
paralytic 125, 131, 132
past lives 32
Petter, Frank Arjava 32, 35–40, 45, 87, 91, 209, 210
physical healing 38, 44, 46, 91, 101, 103, 107, 110, 113, 131–134, 139, 140, 143, 144, 164, 180, 184, 185, 204
placebo 85, 93, 98, 209
power animal 165, 181
prana 50, 76, 82, 83, 84
preaching of repentance 143
primordial Chi 50, 55, 65, 67
Protestant Reiki Master 159
pseudo-science 28, 97
psychic abilities 39, 81, 108
psychic healers 85
psychic surgery 163, 164, 177, 179, 182
psycho-spiritual dangers 156

Q
Qi Gong 39
Qingren, Wang 54
Qumran Literature 118

R
Rabbinic literature 118
Rand, William 29, 157
reiju 43
Reiki 1, 3, 5, 7, 8, 9, 11, 14, 17, 19–51, 55, 57, 60, 61, 65, 67, 68, 70, 71, 74, 86–98, 107, 108, 110, 145, 146, 153–168, 170, 172–189, 192–212
Reiki and Depression 92
Reiki at a distance 93, 168
Reiki Master 17, 21, 25, 27–29, 31, 34, 35, 38, 40, 67, 68, 91, 157–159, 168, 170, 200, 210
Reiki Safety 153
reincarnation 14, 64, 73, 162, 175, 178, 195
Relational Theism 146
relationship with Christ 193
repentance 127, 143, 144, 177, 178, 195–197
Rogers, Martha 83
Rosa, Emily 85, 211
Russell, Terence C. 69, 211

S
Sabbath 140, 141, 142, 143
salvation 40, 44, 47, 109, 110, 111, 113, 123, 124, 132, 134, 140, 143, 147, 161, 175, 178, 184, 189, 190
Sanskrit 29, 37, 38, 57, 76, 82
Schmehr, Robert 94, 211
scientific validation 75, 95, 96, 97
Shakti 156, 167, 207
shaman 23, 33, 55, 86, 180, 209
shamanic crisis 172
shamans 23, 29
Shingon 40, 42, 44
shinrei ryoho 45
Shintoism 44, 47
Shiva 156
side effects 20, 22, 153, 155–157, 165,
Sire, James 147, 211
Skeen, James 81
Son of God 127, 139, 147
sovereignty 116, 126, 186, 188, 191
sozo 109, 110, 134
spirit guides 156, 158, 164, 169, 172, 177, 182

Index

spiritual attack 104, 172
Spiritual Bondage 163
Spiritual Emergency 171
spiritual healing 37, 44, 46, 84, 93, 106, 110, 112, 113, 131, 132, 140, 143, 144, 159, 177, 185
Spiritual Side Effects 156
spiritual transference 45
subtle essence 60, 61
suffering 45, 47, 94, 106, 129, 130, 132, 177, 191, 193
surrender 67, 68, 70, 172, 173, 187, 189
sutra 39, 209
symbols 32, 34, 37, 38, 43, 57, 163, 176, 182

T
Takata, Hawayo 38, 39, 48
Tao 54–68, 70, 206–210
Taoism 40, 41, 47, 53–56, 63–69, 71, 177, 205, 206
Tendai Buddhism 40–44, 208
terminal illnesses 163
The Inner Canon of the Yellow Emperor 51, 52
theism 74, 80, 146, 147, 148, 173
therapeuo 109
therapeutic touch 5, 14
Therapeutic Touch 14, 49, 74–78, 80, 81–86, 89, 96, 97, 208, 209, 211
The Way 61, 65, 67
The Yellow Emperor's Classic of Medicine 53
third eye 36
T'ien-t'ai practice 42, 44
Tipei, John F. 115, 116, 118, 119, 120, 128, 134, 212
Traditional Chinese Medicine 50, 51, 70
transference 45, 48, 116, 119, 153
transformation 22, 60, 67, 145, 161, 167, 172, 207
transpersonal counseling 171, 173
Trinity 62, 111, 175, 209
truth 41, 61, 71, 72, 142, 144, 146, 149, 155, 161–163, 173, 176, 185, 190–194, 196, 197, 204, 206

Tucker, Mary Evelyn 60, 65, 66, 212
Twelftree, Graham H. 130, 134, 139, 140, 212
Tzu, Chuang 53
Tzu, Lao 53, 62

U
ultimate reality 65
Ultimate Reality 70, 72, 148
Universal Energy 32
unruffling 76, 77
upaya 42
Usui, Mikao 36–50, 68, 74, 87, 210

V
vibration 36, 43, 50, 176

W
Wallis, Dr. Ian G. 122, 123, 212
Wang Qingren 54
Warrington, Keith 124, 130, 134, 136, 139, 141, 212
Weldon, John 24, 80, 84, 85, 108, 169, 171, 172, 179, 205, 210
worldview 30, 46, 55, 70–73, 80, 83, 146–148, 157, 161, 165, 171, 173, 175, 190, 206
Wright, Frank Lloyd 73

Y
yin and yang 50–54, 57, 62, 65, 67
yogi 76, 167

About the Author

Originally trained as an English teacher, Dr. Rhonda McClenton has had a variety of career changes, ranging from an educational administrator to forays as a counselor, clinician, and college instructor. Born and raised on the East Coast, she attended both public and private schools where she developed a love for writing and life-long learning. To the end, she graduated with a B.A. from Eastern University in English and Education, an M.Ed. from Temple University in the Psychology of Reading, and a Ph.D. from Trinity Theological Seminary in cooperation with the University of Liverpool with a degree in counseling.

While most of Dr. McClenton's professional life revolved around educating or helping others to advance personally or professionally, attending seminary crystallized her desire to help individuals connect and develop spiritually. Accepting Christ at the age of 13, she has been a passionate follower. In 1999 and 2002, she responded to God's call to ministry and was ordained as a minister where she has taught and counseled.

Around the same time, it was her doctoral research on Reiki, a type of hands-on healing which led her to an environment where Reiki was practiced. Practitioners talked about getting "connected with spirit" or "connecting with God" for healing of the "mind, body, and spirit." Yet, all that she witnessed on this 3-year odyssey was quite different than her experiences and understanding of Christ-based healing. Thus, her work, *Reiki and Christ-based Healing: Differences and Dangers.* is the story behind the original research, designed to teach and inform. What makes her work invaluable is that currently, Reiki and Christ-based healing have never been researched together at the doctoral level with warnings of Reiki's potential dangers.

Dr. McClenton makes her home in Pennsylvania. Interests include writing, biking, and computer technology.

www.ingramcontent.com/pod-product-compliance
Lightning Source LLC
Chambersburg PA
CBHW061259110426
42742CB00012BA/1974